HBR's 10 Must Reads

HBR's 10 Must Reads are definitive collections of classic ideas, practical advice, and essential thinking from the pages of *Harvard Business Review*. Exploring topics like disruptive innovation, emotional intelligence, and new technology in our ever-evolving world, these books empower any leader to make bold decisions and inspire others.

TITLES INCLUDE:

HBR's 10 Must Reads for New Managers
HBR's 10 Must Reads on AI
HBR's 10 Must Reads on Building a Great Culture
HBR's 10 Must Reads on Change Management
HBR's 10 Must Reads on Communication
HBR's 10 Must Reads on Data Strategy
HBR's 10 Must Reads on Decision-Making
HBR's 10 Must Reads on Design Thinking
HBR's 10 Must Reads on Digital Transformation
HBR's 10 Must Reads on Emotional Intelligence
HBR's 10 Must Reads on High Performance
HBR's 10 Must Reads on Innovation
HBR's 10 Must Reads on Leadership
HBR's 10 Must Reads on Leading Winning Teams
HBR's 10 Must Reads on Managing People
HBR's 10 Must Reads on Managing Yourself
HBR's 10 Must Reads on Marketing
HBR's 10 Must Reads on Mental Toughness
HBR's 10 Must Reads on Strategy
HBR's 10 Must Reads on Women and Leadership
HBR's 10 Must Reads Boxed Set (6 books)
HBR's 10 Must Reads Ultimate Boxed Set (14 books)

For a full list, visit hbr.org/mustreads.

HBR's 10 Must Reads

UPDATED & EXPANDED

Managing Yourself

HBR's 10 Must Reads

UPDATED &
EXPANDED

Managing Yourself

Harvard Business Review Press
Boston, Massachusetts

The web addresses referenced in this book were live and correct at the time of the book's publication but may be subject to change.

Library of Congress Cataloging-in-Publication Data

Title: HBR's 10 must reads. Managing yourself
Other titles: HBR's 10 must reads on managing yourself | Managing yourself | Harvard business review.
Description: Updated + expanded [edition]. | Boston, Massachusetts : Harvard Business Review Press, [2025] | Series: HBR's 10 must reads | Includes index.
Identifiers: LCCN 2025015527 (print) | LCCN 2025015528 (ebook) | ISBN 9798892791885 paperback | ISBN 9798892791892 epub
Subjects: LCSH: Management
Classification: LCC HD31 .H3946 2025 (print) | LCC HD31 (ebook) | DDC 650.1—dc23/eng/20250523
LC record available at https://lccn.loc.gov/2025015527
LC ebook record available at https://lccn.loc.gov/2025015528

ISBN: 979-8-89279-188-5
eISBN: 979-8-89279-189-2

The paper used in this publication meets the requirements of the American National Standard for Permanence of Paper for Publications and Documents in Libraries and Archives Z39.48-1992.

Contents

7 **The Hidden Toll of Microstress** 121
Prevent small, difficult moments from
zapping your performance.

by Rob Cross and Karen Dillon

QUICK READ

How to Build a Broader Network Within Your Company 141
Cultivating a growth mindset can help you
make better connections.

by Ko Kuwabara, Jiyin Cao, Soomin Sophie Cho,
and Paul Ingram

8 **How to Navigate Conflict with a Coworker** 149
Seven strategies for working with even the
most difficult people.

by Amy Gallo

QUICK READ

You're Not Powerless in the Face of Impostor Syndrome 161
Four tactics to make moxie your superpower.

by Keith D. Dorsey

9 **Feeling Stuck or Stymied?** 171
To achieve goals that seem out of reach,
try strategic patience.

by Dorie Clark

HBR's 10 Must Reads

UPDATED & EXPANDED

Managing Yourself

1

Managing Oneself

by Peter F. Drucker

History's great achievers—a Napoléon, a da Vinci, a Mozart—have always managed themselves. That, in large measure, is what makes them great achievers. But they are rare exceptions, so unusual both in their talents and their accomplishments as to be considered outside the boundaries of ordinary human existence. Now, most of us, even those of us with modest endowments, will have to learn to manage ourselves. We will have to learn to develop ourselves. We will have to place ourselves where we can make the greatest contribution. And we will have to stay mentally alert and engaged during a 50-year working life, which means knowing how and when to change the work we do.

What Are My Strengths?

Most people think they know what they are good at. They are usually wrong. More often, people know what they are not good at—and even then more people are wrong than right. And yet, a person can perform only from strength. One cannot build performance on weaknesses, let alone on something one cannot do at all.

Throughout history, people had little need to know their strengths. A person was born into a position and a line of work: The peasant's son would also be a peasant; the artisan's daughter, an artisan's wife; and so on. But now people have choices. We need to know our strengths in order to know where we belong.

The only way to discover your strengths is through feedback analysis. Whenever you make a key decision or take a key action, write down what you expect will happen. Nine or 12 months later, compare the actual results with your expectations. I have been practicing this method for 15 to 20 years now, and every time I do it, I am surprised. The feedback analysis showed me, for instance—and to my great surprise—that I have an intuitive understanding of technical people, whether they are engineers or accountants or market researchers. It also showed me that I don't really resonate with generalists.

Feedback analysis is by no means new. It was invented sometime in the 14th century by an otherwise totally obscure German theologian and picked up quite independently, some 150 years later, by John Calvin and Ignatius of Loyola, each of who incorporated it into the practice of his followers. In fact, the steadfast focus on performance and results that this habit produces explains why the institutions these two men founded, the Calvinist church and the Jesuit order, came to dominate Europe within 30 years.

Practiced consistently, this simple method will show you within a fairly short period of time, maybe two or three years, where your strengths lie—and this is the most important thing to know. The method will show you what you are doing or failing to do that deprives you of the full benefits of your strengths.

Idea in Brief

We live in an age of unprecedented opportunity: If you've got ambition, drive, and smarts, you can rise to the top of your chosen profession—regardless of where you started out. But with opportunity comes responsibility. Companies today aren't managing their knowledge workers' careers. Rather, we must each be our own chief executive officer.

Simply put, it's up to you to carve out your place in the work world and know when to change course. And it's up to you to keep yourself engaged and productive during a work life that may span some 50 years. To do all of these things well, you'll need to cultivate a deep understanding of yourself. What are your most valuable strengths and most dangerous weaknesses? Equally important, how do you learn and work with others? What are your most deeply held values? And in what type of work environment can you make the greatest contribution?

The implication is clear: Only when you operate from a combination of your strengths and self-knowledge can you achieve true—and lasting—excellence.

It will show you where you are not particularly competent. And finally, it will show you where you have no strengths and cannot perform.

Several implications for action follow from feedback analysis. First and foremost, concentrate on your strengths. Put yourself where your strengths can produce results.

Second, work on improving your strengths. Analysis will rapidly show where you need to improve skills or acquire new ones. It will also show the gaps in your knowledge—and those can usually be filled. Mathematicians are born, but everyone can learn trigonometry.

Third, discover where your intellectual arrogance is causing disabling ignorance and overcome it. Far too many people—especially people with great expertise in one area—are contemptuous of knowledge in other areas or believe that being bright is a substitute for knowledge. First-rate engineers, for instance, tend to take pride in not knowing anything about people. Human beings, they believe, are much too disorderly for the good engineering mind. Human resources professionals, by contrast, often pride themselves on their ignorance of elementary accounting or of quantitative methods altogether. But taking pride in such ignorance is self-defeating. Go to work on acquiring the skills and knowledge you need to fully realize your strengths.

It is equally essential to remedy your bad habits—the things you do or fail to do that inhibit your effectiveness and performance. Such habits will quickly show up in the feedback. For example, a planner may find that his beautiful plans fail because he does not follow through on them. Like so many brilliant people, he believes that ideas move mountains. But bulldozers move mountains; ideas show where the bulldozers should go to work. This planner will have to learn that the work does not stop when the plan is completed. He must find people to carry out the plan and explain it to them. He must adapt and change it as he puts it into action. And finally, he must decide when to stop pushing the plan.

At the same time, feedback will also reveal when the problem is a lack of manners. Manners are the lubricating oil of an organization. It is a law of nature that two moving bodies in contact with each other create friction. This is as true for human beings as it is for inanimate objects. Manners—simple things like saying "please" and "thank you" and knowing a person's name or asking after her family—enable two people to work together whether they like each other or not. Bright people, especially bright young people, often do not understand this. If analysis shows that someone's brilliant work fails again and again as soon as cooperation from others is required, it probably indicates a lack of courtesy—that is, a lack of manners.

Comparing your expectations with your results also indicates what not to do. We all have a vast number of areas in which we have no talent or skill and little chance of becoming even mediocre. In those areas a person—and especially a knowledge worker—should not take on work, jobs, and assignments. One should waste as little effort as possible on improving areas of low competence. It takes far more energy and work to improve from incompetence to mediocrity than it takes to improve from first-rate performance to excellence. And yet most people—especially most teachers and most organizations—concentrate on making incompetent performers into mediocre ones. Energy, resources, and time should go instead to making a competent person into a star performer.

How Do I Perform?

Amazingly few people know how they get things done. Indeed, most of us do not even know that different people work and perform differently. Too many people work in ways that are not their ways, and that almost guarantees nonperformance. For knowledge workers, How do I perform? may be an even more important question than What are my strengths?

Like one's strengths, how one performs is unique. It is a matter of personality. Whether personality be a matter of nature or nurture, it surely is formed long before a person goes to work. And *how* a person performs is a given, just as *what* a person is good at or not good at is a given. A person's way of performing can be slightly modified, but it is unlikely to be completely changed—and certainly not easily. Just as people achieve results by doing what they are good at, they also achieve results by working in ways that they best perform. A few common personality traits usually determine how a person performs.

Am I a reader or a listener?

The first thing to know is whether you are a reader or a listener. Far too few people even know that there are readers and listeners and that people are rarely both. Even fewer know which of the two they themselves are. But some examples will show how damaging such ignorance can be.

When Dwight Eisenhower was Supreme Commander of the Allied forces in Europe, he was the darling of the press. His press conferences were famous for their style—General Eisenhower showed total command of whatever question he was asked, and he was able to describe a situation and explain a policy in two or three beautifully polished and elegant sentences. Ten years later, the same journalists who had been his admirers held President Eisenhower in open contempt. He never addressed the questions, they complained, but rambled on endlessly about something else. And they constantly ridiculed him for butchering the King's English in incoherent and ungrammatical answers.

Eisenhower apparently did not know that he was a reader, not a listener. When he was supreme commander in Europe, his aides made sure that every question from the press was presented in writing at least half an hour before a conference was to begin. And then Eisenhower was in total command. When he became president, he succeeded two listeners, Franklin D. Roosevelt and Harry Truman. Both men knew themselves to be listeners and both enjoyed free-for-all press conferences. Eisenhower may have felt that he had to do what his two predecessors had done. As a result, he never even heard the questions journalists asked. And Eisenhower is not even an extreme case of a nonlistener.

A few years later, Lyndon Johnson destroyed his presidency, in large measure, by not knowing that he was a listener. His predecessor, John Kennedy, was a reader who had assembled a brilliant group of writers as his assistants, making sure that they wrote to him before discussing their memos in person. Johnson kept these people on his staff—and they kept on writing. He never, apparently, understood one word of what they wrote. Yet as a senator, Johnson had been superb; for parliamentarians have to be, above all, listeners.

Few listeners can be made, or can make themselves, into competent readers—and vice versa. The listener who tries to be a reader will, therefore, suffer the fate of Lyndon Johnson, whereas the reader who tries to be a listener will suffer the fate of Dwight Eisenhower. They will not perform or achieve.

How do I learn?

The second thing to know about how one performs is to know how one learns. Many first-class writers—Winston Churchill is but one example—do poorly in school. They tend to remember their schooling as pure torture. Yet few of their classmates remember it the same way. They may not have enjoyed the school very much, but the worst they suffered was boredom. The explanation is that writers do not, as a rule, learn by listening and reading. They learn by writing. Because schools do not allow them to learn this way, they get poor grades.

Schools everywhere are organized on the assumption that there is only one right way to learn and that it is the same way for everybody. But to be forced to learn the way a school teaches is sheer hell for students who learn differently. Indeed, there are probably half a dozen different ways to learn.

There are people, like Churchill, who learn by writing. Some people learn by taking copious notes. Beethoven, for example, left behind an enormous number of sketchbooks, yet he said he never actually looked at them when he composed. Asked why he kept them, he is reported to have replied, "If I don't write it down immediately, I forget it right away. If I put it into a sketchbook, I never forget it and I never have to look it up again." Some people learn by doing. Others learn by hearing themselves talk.

A chief executive I know who converted a small and mediocre family business into the leading company in its industry was one of those people who learn by talking. He was in the habit of calling his entire senior staff into his office once a week and then talking at them for two or three hours. He would raise policy issues and argue three different positions on each one. He rarely asked his associates for comments or questions; he simply needed an audience to hear himself talk. That's how he learned. And although he is a fairly extreme case, learning through talking is by no means an unusual method. Successful trial lawyers learn the same way, as do many medical diagnosticians (and so do I).

Of all the important pieces of self-knowledge, understanding how you learn is the easiest to acquire. When I ask people, "How do you learn?" most of them know the answer. But when I ask, "Do you act on this knowledge?" few answer yes. And yet, acting on this knowledge is the key to performance; or rather, *not* acting on this knowledge condemns one to nonperformance.

Am I a reader or a listener? and How do I learn? are the first questions to ask. But they are by no means the only ones. To manage yourself effectively, you also have to ask, Do I work well with people, or am I a loner? And if you do work well with people, you then must ask, In what relationship?

Some people work best as subordinates. General George Patton, the great American military hero of World War II, is a prime example. Patton was America's top troop commander. Yet when he was proposed for an independent command, General George Marshall, the U.S. chief of staff—and probably the most successful picker of men in U.S. history—said, "Patton is the best subordinate the American army has ever produced, but he would be the worst commander."

Some people work best as team members. Others work best alone. Some are exceptionally talented as coaches and mentors; others are simply incompetent as mentors.

Another crucial question is, Do I produce results as a decision-maker or as an adviser? A great many people perform best as advisers but cannot take the burden and pressure of making the decision. A good many other people, by contrast, need an adviser to force themselves to think; then they can make decisions and act on them with speed, self-confidence, and courage.

This is a reason, by the way, that the number two person in an organization often fails when promoted to the number one position. The top spot requires a decision-maker. Strong decision-makers often put somebody they trust into the number two spot as their adviser—and in that position the person is outstanding. But in the number one spot, the same person fails. He or she knows what the decision should be but cannot accept the responsibility of actually making it.

Other important questions to ask include, Do I perform well under stress, or do I need a highly structured and predictable environment? Do I work best in a big organization or a small one? Few people work well in all kinds of environments. Again and again, I have seen people who were very successful in large organizations flounder miserably when they moved into smaller ones. And the reverse is equally true.

The conclusion bears repeating: Do not try to change yourself—you are unlikely to succeed. But work hard to improve the way you perform. And try not to take on work you cannot perform or will only perform poorly.

What Are My Values?

To be able to manage yourself, you finally have to ask, What are my values? This is not a question of ethics. With respect to ethics, the rules are the same for everybody, and the test is a simple one. I call it the "mirror test."

In the early years of this century, the most highly respected diplomat of all the great powers was the German ambassador in London. He was clearly destined for great things—to become his country's foreign minister, at least, if not its federal chancellor. Yet in 1906 he abruptly resigned rather than preside over a dinner given by the diplomatic corps for Edward VII. The king was a notorious womanizer and made it clear what kind of dinner he wanted. The ambassador is reported to have said, "I refuse to see a pimp in the mirror in the morning when I shave."

That is the mirror test. Ethics requires that you ask yourself, What kind of person do I want to see in the mirror in the morning? What is ethical behavior in one kind of organization or situation is ethical behavior in another. But ethics is only part of a value system—especially of an organization's value system.

To work in an organization whose value system is unacceptable or incompatible with one's own condemns a person both to frustration and to nonperformance.

Consider the experience of a highly successful human resources executive whose company was acquired by a bigger organization. After the acquisition, she was promoted to do the kind of work she did best, which included selecting people for important positions. The executive deeply believed that a company should hire people for such positions from the outside only after exhausting all the inside possibilities. But her new company believed in first looking outside "to bring in fresh blood." There is something to be said for both approaches—in my experience, the proper one is to do some of both. They are, however, fundamentally incompatible—not as policies but as values. They bespeak different views of the relationship between organizations and people; different views of the responsibility of an organization to its people and their development; and different views of a person's most important contribution to an enterprise. After several years of frustration, the executive quit—at considerable financial loss. Her values and the values of the organization simply were not compatible.

Similarly, whether a pharmaceutical company tries to obtain results by making constant, small improvements or by achieving occasional, highly expensive, and risky "breakthroughs" is not primarily an economic question. The results of either strategy may be pretty much the same. At bottom, there is a conflict between a value system that sees the company's contribution in terms of helping physicians do better what they already do and a value system that is oriented toward making scientific discoveries.

Whether a business should be run for short-term results or with a focus on the long term is likewise a question of values. Financial analysts believe that businesses can be run for both simultaneously. Successful businesspeople know better. To be sure, every company has to produce short-term results. But in any conflict between short-term results and long-term growth, each company will determine its own priority. This is not primarily a disagreement about economics. It is fundamentally a value conflict regarding the function of a business and the responsibility of management.

Value conflicts are not limited to business organizations. One of the fastest-growing pastoral churches in the United States measures success by the number of new parishioners. Its leadership believes that what matters is how many newcomers join the congregation. The Good Lord will then minister to their spiritual needs or at least to the needs of a sufficient percentage. Another pastoral, evangelical church believes that what matters is people's spiritual growth. The church eases out newcomers who join but do not enter into its spiritual life.

Again, this is not a matter of numbers. At first glance, it appears that the second church grows more slowly. But it retains a far larger proportion of newcomers than the first one does. Its growth, in other words, is more solid. This is also not a theological problem, or only secondarily so. It is a problem about values. In a public debate, one pastor argued, "Unless you first come to church, you will never find the gate to the Kingdom of Heaven."

"No," answered the other. "Until you first look for the gate to the Kingdom of Heaven, you don't belong in church."

Organizations, like people, have values. To be effective in an organization, a person's values must be compatible with the organization's values. They do not need to be the same, but they must be close enough to coexist. Otherwise, the person will not only be frustrated but also will not produce results.

A person's strengths and the way that person performs rarely conflict; the two are complementary. But there is sometimes a conflict between a person's values and his or her strengths. What one does well—even very well and successfully—may not fit with one's value system. In that case, the work may not appear to be worth devoting one's life to (or even a substantial portion thereof).

If I may, allow me to interject a personal note. Many years ago, I too had to decide between my values and what I was doing successfully. I was doing very well as a young investment banker in London in the mid-1930s, and the work clearly fit my strengths. Yet I did not see myself making a contribution as an asset manager. People, I realized, were what I valued, and I saw no point in being the richest man in the cemetery. I had no money and no other job prospects. Despite the continuing Depression, I quit—and it was the right thing to do. Values, in other words, are and should be the ultimate test.

Where Do I Belong?

A small number of people know very early where they belong. Mathematicians, musicians, and cooks, for instance, are usually mathematicians, musicians, and cooks by the time they are four or five years old. Physicians usually decide on their careers in their teens, if not earlier. But most people, especially highly gifted people, do not really know where they belong until they are well past their mid-twenties. By that time, however, they should know the answers to the three questions: What are my strengths? How do I perform? and, What are my values? And then they can and should decide where they belong.

Or rather, they should be able to decide where they do *not* belong. The person who has learned that he or she does not perform well in a big organization should have learned to say no to a position in one. The person who has learned that he or she is not a decision-maker should have learned to say no to a decision-making assignment. A General Patton (who probably never learned this himself) should have learned to say no to an independent command.

Equally important, knowing the answer to these questions enables a person to say to an opportunity, an offer, or an assignment, "Yes, I will do that. But this is the way I should be doing it. This is the way it should be structured. This is the way the relationships should be. These are the kind of results you should expect from me, and in this time frame, because this is who I am."

Successful careers are not planned. They develop when people are prepared for opportunities because they know their strengths, their method of work, and their values. Knowing where one belongs can transform an ordinary person—hardworking and competent but otherwise mediocre—into an outstanding performer.

What Should I Contribute?

Throughout history, the great majority of people never had to ask the question, What should I contribute? They were told what to contribute, and their tasks were dictated either by the work itself—as it was for the peasant or artisan—or by a master or a mistress—as it was for domestic servants. And until very recently, it was taken for granted that most people were subordinates who did as they were told. Even in the 1950s and 1960s, the new knowledge workers (the so-called organization men) looked to their company's personnel department to plan their careers.

Then in the late 1960s, no one wanted to be told what to do any longer. Young men and women began to ask, What do *I* want to do? And what they heard was that the way to contribute was to "do your own thing." But this solution was as wrong as the organization men's had been. Very few of the people who believed that doing one's own thing would lead to contribution, self-fulfillment, and success achieved any of the three.

But still, there is no return to the old answer of doing what you are told or assigned to do. Knowledge workers in particular have to learn to ask a question that has not been asked before: What *should* my contribution be? To answer it, they must address three distinct elements: What does the situation require? Given my strengths, my way of performing, and my values, how can I make the greatest contribution to what needs to be done? And finally, What results have to be achieved to make a difference?

Consider the experience of a newly appointed hospital administrator. The hospital was big and prestigious, but it had been coasting on its reputation for 30 years. The new administrator decided that his contribution should be to establish a standard of excellence in one important area within two years. He chose to focus on the emergency room, which was big, visible, and sloppy. He decided that every patient who came into the ER had to be seen by a qualified nurse within 60 seconds. Within 12 months, the hospital's emergency room had become a model for all hospitals in the United States, and within another two years, the whole hospital had been transformed.

As this example suggests, it is rarely possible—or even particularly fruitful—to look too far ahead. A plan can usually cover no more than 18 months and still be reasonably clear and specific. So the question in most cases should be, Where and how can I achieve results that will make a difference within the next year and a half? The answer must balance several things. First, the results should be hard to achieve—they should require "stretching," to use the current buzzword. But also, they should be within reach. To aim at results that cannot be achieved—or that can be only under the most unlikely circumstances—is not being ambitious; it is being foolish. Second, the results should be meaningful. They should make a difference. Finally, results should be visible and, if at all possible, measurable. From this will come a course of action: what to do, where and how to start, and what goals and deadlines to set.

Responsibility for Relationships

Very few people work by themselves and achieve results by themselves—a few great artists, a few great scientists, a few great athletes. Most people work with others and are effective with other people. That is true whether they are members of an organization or independently employed. Managing yourself requires taking responsibility for relationships. This has two parts.

The first is to accept the fact that other people are as much individuals as you yourself are. They perversely insist on behaving like human beings. This means that they too have their strengths; they too have their ways of getting things done; they too have their values. To be effective, therefore, you have to know the strengths, the performance modes, and the values of your coworkers.

That sounds obvious, but few people pay attention to it. Typical is the person who was trained to write reports in his or her first assignment because that boss was a reader. Even if the next boss is a listener, the person goes on writing reports that, invariably, produce no results. Invariably the boss will think the employee is stupid, incompetent, and lazy, and he or she will fail. But that could have been avoided if the employee had only looked at the new boss and analyzed how *this* boss performs.

Bosses are neither a title on the organization chart nor a "function." They are individuals and are entitled to do their work in the way they do it best. It is incumbent on the people who work with them to observe them, to find out how they work, and to adapt themselves to what makes their bosses most effective. This, in fact, is the secret of "managing" the boss.

The same holds true for all your coworkers. Each works his or her way, not your way. And each is entitled to work in his or her way. What matters is whether they perform and what their values are. As for how they perform—each is likely to do it differently. The first secret of effectiveness is to understand the people you work with and depend on so that you can make use of their strengths, their ways of working, and their values. Working relationships are as much based on the people as they are on the work.

The second part of relationship responsibility is taking responsibility for communication. Whenever I, or any other consultant, start to work with an organization, the first thing I hear about are all the personality conflicts. Most of these arise from the fact that people do not know what other people are doing and how they do their work, or what contribution the other people are concentrating on and what results they expect. And the reason they do not know is that they have not asked and therefore have not been told.

This failure to ask reflects human stupidity less than it reflects human history. Until recently, it was unnecessary to tell any of these things to anybody. In the medieval city, everyone in a district plied the same trade. In the countryside, everyone in a valley planted the same crop as soon as the frost was out of the ground. Even those few people who did things that were not "common" worked alone, so they did not have to tell anyone what they were doing.

Today the great majority of people work with others who have different tasks and responsibilities. The marketing vice president may have come out of sales and know everything about sales, but she knows nothing about the things she has never done—pricing, advertising, packaging, and the like. So the people who do these things must make sure that the marketing vice president understands what they are trying to do, why they are trying to do it, how they are going to do it, and what results to expect.

If the marketing vice president does not understand what these high-grade knowledge specialists are doing, it is primarily their fault, not hers. They have not educated her. Conversely, it is the marketing vice president's responsibility to make sure that all of her coworkers understand how she looks at marketing: what her goals are, how she works, and what she expects of herself and of each one of them.

Even people who understand the importance of taking responsibility for relationships often do not communicate sufficiently with their associates. They are afraid of being thought presumptuous or inquisitive or stupid. They are wrong. Whenever someone goes to his or her associates and says, "This is what I am good at. This is how I work. These are my values. This is the contribution I plan to concentrate on and the results I should be expected to deliver," the response is always, "This is most helpful. But why didn't you tell me earlier?"

And one gets the same reaction—without exception, in my experience—if one continues by asking, "And what do I need to know about your strengths, how you perform, your values, and your proposed contribution?" In fact, knowledge workers should request this of everyone with whom they work, whether as subordinate, superior, colleague, or team member. And again, whenever this is done, the reaction is always, "Thanks for asking me. But why didn't you ask me earlier?"

Organizations are no longer built on force but on trust. The existence of trust between people does not necessarily mean that they like one another. It means that they understand one another. Taking responsibility for relationships is therefore an absolute necessity. It is a duty. Whether one is a member of the organization, a consultant to it, a supplier, or a distributor, one owes that responsibility to all one's coworkers: those whose work one depends on as well as those who depend on one's own work.

The Second Half of Your Life

When work for most people meant manual labor, there was no need to worry about the second half of your life. You simply kept on doing what you had always done. And if you were lucky enough to survive 40 years of hard work in the mill or on the railroad, you were quite happy to spend the rest of your life doing nothing. Today, however, most work is knowledge work, and knowledge workers are not "finished" after 40 years on the job, they are merely bored.

We hear a great deal of talk about the midlife crisis of the executive. It is mostly boredom. At 45, most executives have reached the peak of their business careers, and they know it. After 20 years of doing very much the same kind of work, they are very good at their jobs. But they are not learning or contributing or deriving challenge and satisfaction from the job. And yet they are still likely to face another 20 if not 25 years of work. That is why managing oneself increasingly leads one to begin a second career.

There are three ways to develop a second career. The first is actually to start one. Often this takes nothing more than moving from one kind of organization to another: the divisional controller in a large corporation, for instance, becomes the controller of a medium-sized hospital. But there are also growing numbers of people who move into different lines of work altogether: the business executive or government official who enters the ministry at 45, for instance; or the midlevel manager who leaves corporate life after 20 years to attend law school and become a small-town attorney.

We will see many more second careers undertaken by people who have achieved modest success in their first jobs. Such people have substantial skills, and they know how to work. They need a community—the house is empty with the children gone—and they need income as well. But above all, they need challenge.

The second way to prepare for the second half of your life is to develop a parallel career. Many people who are very successful in their first careers stay in the work they have been doing, either on a full-time or part-time or consulting basis. But in addition, they create a parallel job, usually in a nonprofit organization, that takes another 10 hours of work a week. They might take over the administration of their church, for instance, or the presidency of the local Girl Scouts council. They might run the battered women's shelter, work as a children's librarian for the local public library, sit on the school board, and so on.

Finally, there are the social entrepreneurs. These are usually people who have been very successful in their first careers. They love their work, but it no longer challenges them. In many cases they keep on doing what they have been doing all along but spend less and less of their time on it. They also start another activity, usually a nonprofit. My friend Bob Buford, for example, built a very successful television company that he still runs. But he has also founded and built a successful nonprofit organization that works with Protestant churches, and he is building another to teach social entrepreneurs how to manage their own nonprofit ventures while still running their original businesses.

People who manage the second half of their lives may always be a minority. The majority may "retire on the job" and count the years until their actual retirement. But it is this minority, the men and women who see a long working-life expectancy as an opportunity both for themselves and for society, who will become leaders and models.

There is one prerequisite for managing the second half of your life: You must begin long before you enter it. When it first became clear 30 years ago that working-life expectancies were lengthening very fast, many observers (including myself) believed that retired people would increasingly become volunteers for nonprofit institutions. That has not happened. If one does not begin to volunteer before one is 40 or so, one will not volunteer once past 60.

Similarly, all the social entrepreneurs I know began to work in their chosen second enterprise long before they reached their peak in their original business. Consider the example of a successful lawyer, the legal counsel to a large corporation, who has started a venture to establish model schools in his state. He began to do volunteer legal work for the schools when he was around 35. He was elected to the school board at age 40. At age 50, when he had amassed a fortune, he started his own enterprise to build and to run model schools. He is, however, still working nearly full-time as the lead counsel in the company he helped found as a young lawyer.

There is another reason to develop a second major interest, and to develop it early. No one can expect to live very long without experiencing a serious setback in his or her life or work. There is the competent engineer who is passed over for promotion at age 45. There is the competent college professor who realizes at age 42 that she will never get a professorship at a big university,

even though she may be fully qualified for it. There are trage-
dies in one's family life: the breakup of one's marriage or the
loss of a child. At such times, a second major interest—not just a
hobby—may make all the difference. The engineer, for example,
now knows that he has not been very successful in his job. But
in his outside activity—as church treasurer, for example—he is a
success. One's family may break up, but in that outside activity
there is still a community.

In a society in which success has become so terribly important, having options will become increasingly vital. Historically,
there was no such thing as "success." The overwhelming majority of people did not expect anything but to stay in their "proper
station," as an old English prayer has it. The only mobility was
downward mobility.

In a knowledge society, however, we expect everyone to be a
success. This is clearly an impossibility. For a great many people,
there is at best an absence of failure. Wherever there is success,
there has to be failure. And then it is vitally important for the
individual, and equally for the individual's family, to have an
area in which he or she can contribute, make a difference, and
be *somebody*. That means finding a second area—whether in a
second career, a parallel career, or a social venture—that offers
an opportunity for being a leader, for being respected, for being
a success.

The challenges of managing oneself may seem obvious, if not
elementary. And the answers may seem self-evident to the point
of appearing naive. But managing oneself requires new and unprecedented things from the individual, and especially from the
knowledge worker. In effect, managing oneself demands that
each knowledge worker think and behave like a chief executive
officer. Further, the shift from manual workers who do as they

are told to knowledge workers who have to manage themselves profoundly challenges social structure. Every existing society, even the most individualistic one, takes two things for granted, if only subconsciously: that organizations outlive workers, and that most people stay put.

But today the opposite is true. Knowledge workers outlive organizations, and they are mobile. The need to manage oneself is therefore creating a revolution in human affairs.

Originally published in January 2005. Reprint R0501K

You Don't Find Your Purpose—You Build It

by John Coleman

How do I find my purpose?"

Ever since Daniel Gulati, Oliver Segovia, and I published *Passion and Purpose* six years ago, I've received hundreds of questions—from younger and older people alike—about purpose. We're all looking for it. Most of us feel that we've never found it, we've lost it, or in some way we're falling short.

But in the midst of all this angst, we're also suffering from what I see as fundamental misconceptions about purpose—neatly encapsulated by the question I receive most frequently: "How do I find my purpose?" Challenging these misconceptions could help us all develop a more rounded vision of it.

Misconception 1: Purpose is only a thing you find

On social media, I often see an inspiring quotation attributed to Mark Twain: "The two most important days in your life are the day you are born and the day you find out why." It neatly articulates what I'll call the "Hollywood version" of purpose. Like Neo in *The Matrix* or Rey in *Star Wars*, we're all just moving through life waiting until fate delivers a higher calling to us.

Make no mistake: That can happen, at least in some form. I recently saw Scott Harrison of Charity: Water speak, and in many ways his story was about how he found a higher purpose after a period of wandering. But I think it's rarer than most people think. For the average 20-year-old in college or 40-year-old in an unfulfilling job, searching for the silver bullet to give life meaning is more likely to end in frustration than fulfillment.

In achieving professional purpose, most of us have to focus as much on *making* our work meaningful as in *taking* meaning from it. Put differently, purpose is a thing you build, not a thing you find. Almost any work can possess remarkable purpose. School bus drivers bear enormous responsibility—caring for and keeping safe dozens of children—and are an essential part of ensuring our children receive the education they need and deserve. Nurses play an essential role not simply in treating people's medical conditions but also in guiding them through some of life's most difficult times. Cashiers can be a friendly, uplifting interaction in someone's day—often desperately needed—or a forgettable or regrettable one. But in each of these instances, purpose is often primarily derived from focusing on what's so meaningful about the job and on doing it in such a way that that meaning is enhanced and takes center stage. Sure, some jobs more naturally lend themselves to senses of meaning, but many require at least some deliberate effort to invest them with the purpose we seek.

Misconception 2: Purpose is a single thing

The second misconception I often hear is that purpose can be articulated as a single thing. Some people genuinely do seem to have an overwhelming purpose in their lives. Mother Teresa

Idea in Brief

The Problem

Many people struggle with their personal purpose, believing it is something they should discover. This mindset can lead to frustration and a lack of direction.

The Solution

Purpose is not found; it is built through intentional action. Identify your core values and passions, set clear goals that align with them, take deliberate steps toward achieving them, and continuously refine your purpose as you evolve.

The Payoff

People who continually build their purpose over time are more likely to experience greater satisfaction and success.

lived her life to serve the poor. Marie Curie devoted her energy to her work. Samuel Johnson poured every part of himself into his writing.

And yet even these luminaries had other sources of purpose in their lives. Mother Teresa served the poor as part of what she believed was a higher calling. Curie, the Nobel Prize–winning scientist, was also a devoted wife and mother (she wrote a biography of her husband, Pierre, and one of her daughters, Irene, won her own Nobel Prize). And Johnson, beyond his writing, was known to be a great humanitarian in his community, often caring personally for the poor.

Most of us will have multiple sources of purpose in our lives. For me, I find it in my children, my marriage, my faith, my writing, my work, and my community. For almost everyone, there's no one thing we can find. It's not *purpose* but *purposes* we are looking for—the multiple sources of meaning that help us find value in our work and lives. Professional commitments are only one component of this meaning, and often our work isn't central to our purpose but a means to helping others, including our families and communities. Acknowledging these multiple sources of purpose takes the pressure off finding a single thing to give our lives meaning.

Misconception 3: Purpose is stable over time

It's common now for people to have multiple careers in their lifetimes. I know one individual, for example, who recently left a successful private equity career to found a startup. I know two more people who recently left business careers to run for elective office. And whether or not we switch professional commitments, most of us will experience personal phases in which our sources of meaning change—childhood, young adulthood, parenthood, and empty-nesting, to name a few.

This evolution in our sources of purpose isn't flaky or demonstrative of a lack of commitment, but natural and good. Just as we all find meaning in multiple places, the sources of that meaning can and do change over time. My sense of purpose at 20 was dramatically different in many ways than it is now, and the same could be said of almost anyone you meet.

How do you find your purpose? That's the wrong question to ask. We should be looking to endow everything we do with purpose, to allow for the multiple sources of meaning that will naturally develop in our lives, and to be comfortable with those changing over time. Unpacking what we mean by "purpose" can allow us to better understand its presence and role in our lives.

Adapted from hbr.org, October 20, 2017. Reprint H03YZX

How to Define, Develop, and Communicate Your Personal Brand

by Rachel Montañez

W hether you like it or not, you're building a personal brand.

Your personal brand is the combination of your skills, the values you present, and the impression you leave on others. While actively building your personal brand may seem like a selfish endeavor, it's far from it. It's an empowering choice, one that can give you control over your professional development, network, career, and overall well-being. It can even make you more visible—and therefore, more satisfied—in your current job.

Like anything in your career, however, building your brand isn't a onetime effort. It will take time and energy, and it requires consistent upkeep. Thankfully, there are actions you can take daily to help you define, develop, and communicate your personal brand.

Define Your Brand

It's impossible to have a strong personal brand if you don't have a good grasp on who you are, what you enjoy, and what you're good at. These things will most likely change over time, which is why defining your brand is something you can, and should, do often. Here's how:

1. Tune in to your emotions

Emotions are powerful, and they can tell you a lot about yourself and your interests. At the end of each day, or after peak moments where your feelings are heightened, take a minute to be mindful. Choose a word or two that best matches how you feel and write it down. The goal is to tune in to how you relate to your different work tasks, activities, or even colleagues. This practice can also help you gain more confidence in the tasks you're good at, understand and express your desires, and better prepare for interactions that don't align with your values.

For example, let's say you've just left a meeting that could've been completed in 15 minutes instead of 30. You note that this made you feel frustrated. That's a signal that you value efficiency. Being a problem solver who maximizes time and effort could become part of your personal brand. Next time you're leading a meeting, you might write out an agenda and the end goal and then share it with attendees beforehand so that everyone stays on track. During the meeting itself, prioritize moving things along when the group gets stuck or the focus wanders.

2. Find your stakeholders

We aren't always the best judge of ourselves—that's why we need stakeholders. Think of your stakeholders as the people inside

Idea in Brief

The Challenge

Standing out in your career requires more than just having skills and experience. Developing, and effectively communicating, your personal brand is essential to advance and succeed.

The Solution

A strong brand is built on clarity about your strengths, values, and unique selling points. Think about what you're good at and what you want to do, then seek out assignments and career paths that align with that. Use various platforms, such as social media, networking events, and professional portfolios, to consistently convey your brand message.

The Payoff

A well-defined and well-communicated brand can increase your visibility, enhance your professional opportunities, and strengthen your reputation.

your company who have an interest in your success and how well you do your job. They're the people you can always go to for an objective opinion or a supportive pep talk—your manager, mentor, sponsor, or even just a close colleague.

When you meet with them, ask for feedback. You could say, "I really value our relationship. In what ways do I bring value to you?" Or, "How would you describe me?" Their answers may give you a better understanding of how others see you and the personal brand you're currently portraying. You can make adjustments if their view doesn't match the brand you're aiming for.

If you feel like you're not getting the feedback you need, you can also bring new stakeholders in and phase others out. This can help you gain further visibility and make sure you're respectful of each person's time. Ask yourself: Who is providing me with helpful insights, and where can I redirect my energy so that both parties mutually benefit from our relationship?

3. Understand your skills

It's important to regularly reflect on your current skill set and how you're using it to make an impact. After all, your skills are core to who you are and your personal brand. On a weekly basis, or after completing a project of interest, consider the skills that made your work possible. Ask yourself: What skills do I use daily to achieve results? What am I most known for? How might those skills evolve in the future? Which ones helped me achieve success on this project?

This is also another great place to deploy your stakeholders. If you're not getting regular feedback, you won't have an accurate, contextual measure of your skills and how to develop them. To get the conversation going, you can say something like, "What did I do well [during this project], and where could I have done even better?"

Develop Your Brand

Defining and continuing to redefine your personal brand is only the first step. Your personal brand is most impactful when others can see it in action. The best place to start showcasing your brand, and developing it further, is through your daily actions at work.

1. Keep outcomes in mind

When you're doing a task, always think about the outcome that will best boost your personal brand. Let that outcome guide how you complete the work.

For example, say part of your personal brand is being seen as a leader. An outcome that would help you boost that part of your brand is to be put in charge of a cross-functional project. Your approach to your daily work should be in service of that outcome. Show others your propensity for leadership by stepping up on your current team. Ask smart questions and speak up when you see a better approach. You can also help break down silos across business units by regularly meeting with peers or leaders from other departments to understand how your work overlaps and create shared goals. These actions will help ensure you're embodying your personal brand on a daily basis and will help others see it, too.

2. Improve the organization

Look for things that need improving in your organization that align with your brand, and take action. For example, perhaps others have described you as a social butterfly, and you've begun to see this as part of your brand. The positive relationships you've formed give you influence, and you can use that to make change happen inside your organization.

Maybe your company's executives are passionate about corporate sustainability, but employee participation is down on a related company initiative. To further develop your brand as an influencer and leader, find ways to drive awareness and encourage your peers to participate. This will further bolster your personal brand while driving valuable change internally.

3. Become a stakeholder

Having your own personal stakeholders is important, but so is being one for others. Look for opportunities to share your knowledge and develop other people. Doing so helps you strengthen your network, gain visibility, learn more about yourself, and further develop your brand.

For example, maybe you're eager to share tips on how to work smarter and save time on tedious tasks. You may discover that part of the brand you're building is being seen as someone who is productive and always delivers quick results.

Sharing your advice with others is also simply a kind thing to do—and it's never bad to have kindness be part of your brand. Extending kindness has scientific well-being and happiness benefits that can positively affect your mental health.

Communicate Your Brand

You've defined your brand. You've developed it further within your organization. Now it's time to make sure everyone knows who you are and what you stand for. Here's how to regularly make sure your personal brand doesn't go unnoticed:

1. Share your story

Communicating your personal brand through social media, especially on platforms like LinkedIn, can help you gain visibility among your colleagues, your company's executives, and recruiters. One great way to use this platform is to share stories about the skills and talents core to your personal brand that may not be so obvious on your résumé or in your day-to-day work. PwC's 2023 Global Hopes and Fears study found that 35% of people believe they have skills that aren't clear from their qualifications, job history, or job titles. Further, 46% agreed that employers focus too much on job history and not enough on skills when hiring.

To make your skills shine, don't be afraid to get personal by sharing talents you've built outside work. For example, say you're a litigator with a side passion as an Etsy vendor. You can share the story of how you've built persuasive writing skills through advertising, creativity that helps you think quickly on your feet, and a growth mindset that allows you to see the big picture. Your interests can and should be part of your personal brand, too. The things you do outside of work typically make you a more well-rounded person, and that in turn makes you more competitive.

If you're trying to reach a wider audience beyond your personal network, ask your human resources department if they're looking for any employee experience stories to help with talent acquisition or employer branding. You can use this opportunity to share a success story that shows your personal brand in action. Not only will sharing your story help you communicate your brand to a larger network—it will also help increase your visibility internally, improve your storytelling skills, and give you the chance to collaborate with others outside of your function.

2. Skip the empty small talk

To make yourself and your personal brand more visible, you need to network. But that doesn't mean you should lean into boring small talk. For example, when someone asks, "How are you?" fight the urge to reply with the typical "Good, and you?" Use the opportunity to talk about your work and highlight your personal brand. Say something like: "I'm well, thanks, and looking forward to the week ahead! I'm working on [a new project], and I'm really excited about [the impact it will have] and [the skills I'm building]. I'd love to talk to you about it more if you're interested. But first, how are things with you?"

Before any planned encounters, try to write down two or three projects, life updates, or personal wins that you're eager to share. This can help you stay focused on communicating your brand and go beyond the small talk.

3. Celebrate others

Great brands aren't one-sided—yours shouldn't be either. It's important to recognize and celebrate others for their achievements as much as you celebrate your own. When a coworker or connection reaches a new work milestone, show your support with a social media shout-out, a personal email, or even a card. Beyond being a nice thing to do, it can have many benefits for you and your personal brand. It's a great way to stay connected to your colleagues and ensure you stay top of mind for them. Just like when you share your knowledge and skills, celebrating others will encourage them to celebrate you when you've achieved something, further boosting your brand.

You also don't have to limit these interactions to celebratory moments. If you find things that resonate with you in someone else's posts, reshare their update, comment, or reach out with resources you've found helpful. When it comes to building a personal brand, compassion will always be a good addition.

. . .

Building your brand is an ongoing process, and it's important to always be on the lookout for things that may stand in your way—burnout, perfectionism, and perhaps more. But remember: You don't have to do and be everything. Be true to you. That's the highest form of self-care and the most sustainable way to build your personal brand.

Adapted from hbr.org, September 4, 2023. Reprint H07S9U

2

Building an Ethical Career

by Maryam Kouchaki and Isaac H. Smith

Most of us think of ourselves as good people. We set out to be ethical, and we hope that in pivotal moments we will rise to the occasion. But when it comes to building an ethical career, good intentions are insufficient. Decades' worth of research has identified social and psychological processes and biases that cloud people's moral judgment, leading them to violate their own values and often to create contorted, post hoc justifications for their behavior. So how can you ensure that from day to day and decade to decade you will do the right thing in your professional life?

The first step requires shifting to a mindset we term *moral humility*—the recognition that we all have the capacity to transgress if we're not vigilant. Moral humility pushes people to admit that temptations, rationalizations, and situations can lead even the best of us to misbehave, and it encourages them to think of ethics as not only avoiding the bad but also pursuing the good. It helps them see this sort of character development as a lifelong pursuit. We've been conducting research on morality and ethics in the workplace for more than a decade, and on the basis of our own and others' findings, we suggest that people who want to develop ethical careers should consider a three-stage approach: (1) Prepare in advance for moral challenges; (2) make good decisions in the moment; and (3) reflect on and learn from moral successes and failures.

Planning to Be Good

Preparing for ethical challenges is important, because people are often well aware of what they *should* do when thinking about the future but tend to focus on what they *want* to do in the present. This tendency to overestimate the virtuousness of our future selves is part of what Ann Tenbrunsel of Notre Dame and colleagues call the *ethical mirage.*

Counteracting this bias begins with understanding your personal strengths and weaknesses. What are your values? When are you most likely to violate them? In his book *The Road to Character*, David Brooks distinguishes between *résumé* virtues (skills, abilities, and accomplishments that you can put on your résumé, such as "increased ROI by 10% on a multimillion-dollar project") and *eulogy* virtues (things people praise you for after you've died, such as being a loyal friend, kind, and a hard worker). Although the two categories may overlap, résumé virtues often relate to what you've done for yourself, whereas eulogy virtues relate to the person you are and what you've done for others—that is, your character.

Idea in Brief

Most of us think of ourselves as good people. We set out to be ethical at work, and we hope that in pivotal moments we will rise to the occasion. But when it comes to building an ethical career, good intentions are insufficient. Decades' worth of research has identified psychological processes and biases that cloud people's moral judgment, leading them to violate their own values, and often to create contorted, post hoc justifications for their behavior.

How can we ensure that we will consistently do the right thing in our professional lives? By shifting our mindset to one of moral humility, recognizing that we all have the capacity for ethical transgressions if we aren't vigilant. The authors suggest a three-stage approach for staying on the straight and narrow: Prepare in advance for moral challenges, including instituting proper safeguards; make good decisions in the moment; and reflect on and learn from moral successes and failures.

So ask yourself: What eulogy virtues am I trying to develop? Or, as the management guru Peter Drucker asked, "What do you want to be remembered for?" and "What do you want to contribute?" Framing your professional life as a quest for contribution rather than achievement can fundamentally change the way you approach your career. And it's helpful to consider those questions early, before you develop mindsets, habits, and routines that are resistant to change.

Goal setting can also lay the groundwork for ethical behavior. Professionals regularly set targets for many aspects of their work and personal lives, yet few think to approach ethics in this way. Benjamin Franklin famously wrote in his autobiography about trying to master 13 traits he identified as essential for a virtuous life (including industry, justice, and humility). He even created a chart to track his daily progress. We don't suggest that everyone engage in similarly rigid documentation, but we do suggest that you sit down and write out eulogy-virtue goals that are challenging but attainable. That is similar to what Clayton Christensen of Harvard Business School advocates for in chapter 10 of this book. After battling cancer, Christensen decided that the metric that mattered most to him was "the individual people whose lives I've touched."

Even the most carefully constructed goals, however, are still just good intentions. They must be fortified by personal safeguards—that is, habits and tendencies that have been shown to bring out people's better angels. For instance, studies suggest that quality sleep, personal prayer (for the religious), and mindfulness can help people manage and strengthen their self-control and resist temptation at work.

We also recommend "if-then planning"—what the psychologist Peter Gollwitzer calls *implementation intentions*. Dozens of research studies have shown that this practice ("If X happens, then I will do Y") can be effective in changing people's behavior, especially when such plans are voiced aloud. They can be simple but must also be specific, tying a situational cue (a trigger) to a desired behavior. For example: *If* my boss asks me to do something potentially unethical, *then* I will turn to a friend or a mentor outside the organization for advice before acting. *If* I am solicited for a bribe, *then* I will consult my company's legal team and formal policies for guidance. *If* I witness sexual harassment or racial prejudice, *then* I will immediately stand up for the victim. Making if-then plans tailored to your strengths, weaknesses, values, and circumstances can help protect you against lapses in self-control, or inaction when action is required. But be sure to make your if-then plans *before* you encounter the situation—preparation is key.

Mentors, too, can help you avoid ethical missteps. When expanding your professional network and developing relationships with advisers, don't look only for those who can hasten your climb up the career ladder; also consider who might be able to support you when it comes to moral decisions. Build connections with people inside and outside your organization whose values are similar to yours and whom you can ask for ethics-related advice. Both of us have reached out to mentors for advice on ethical issues, and we teach our MBA students to do the same. Having a supportive network—and particularly a trusted ethical mentor—may also bring you opportunities to make a positive impact in your career.

Once you've made a commitment to living an ethical life, don't be shy about letting people know it. No one likes a holier-than-thou attitude, but subtle moral signaling can be helpful, particularly when it's directed at colleagues. You can do this by openly discussing potential moral challenges and how you would want to react or by building a reputation for doing things the right way. For example, in a study one of us (Maryam) conducted, participants were much less likely to ask an online partner to engage in unethical behavior after receiving an email from that partner with a virtuous quotation in the signature line (such as "Success without honor is worse than fraud").

Direct conversation can be tricky, given that people are often hesitant to discuss ethically charged issues. But if you think it's possible, we recommend engaging your coworkers, because ambiguity is a breeding ground for self-interested rationalization. Tactfully ask clarifying questions and make your own expectations clear: for example, "I think it's important that we don't cross any ethical lines here."

We are all shaped more by our environment than we realize, so it's also critical to choose a workplace that will allow if not encourage you to behave ethically. Not surprisingly, employees who feel that their needs, abilities, and values fit well with their organization tend to be more satisfied and motivated than their misaligned peers, and they perform better. Of course, many factors go into choosing a job—but in general people tend to overemphasize traditional metrics such as compensation and promotion opportunities and underemphasize the importance of the right *moral* fit. Our work and that of others has shown that ethical stress is a strong predictor of employee fatigue, decreased job satisfaction, lower motivation, and increased turnover.

Some industries seem to have cultural norms that are more or less amenable to dishonesty. In one study, when employees of a large international bank were reminded of their professional identity, they tended to cheat more, on average, than non-banker counterparts given the same reminder. This is not to say, of course, that all bankers are unethical, or that only unethical people should pursue careers in banking (although it does highlight how important it is for banks to prioritize hiring morally upstanding employees). We do suggest, however, that anyone starting a new job should learn about the organization and the relevant industry so as to prepare for morally compromising situations. Job interviews often conclude with the candidate's being asked, "Do you have any questions for me?" A possible response is "What types of ethical dilemmas might be faced in this job?" or "What does this company do to promote ethical business practices?"

Research also shows that elements of a work environment can enhance or diminish self-control, regardless of cultural norms: High uncertainty, excessive cognitive demands, long days and late nights, and consecutive stretch goals all correlate with increased rates of unethical behavior. Such pressures may wax and wane over time in your workplace, but during periods of intensity you should be extra vigilant.

Making Good Decisions

Even if you've planned for an ethical career and established safeguards, it can be difficult to face moral challenges in the moment. Sometimes people overlook the implications of their decisions—or they find fanciful ways of rationalizing immoral, self-interested behavior. In other instances, they face quandaries in which the right decision isn't obvious—for example, a choice between loyalty to one's coworkers and loyalty to a customer, or a proposed solution that will produce both positive and negative externalities, such as good jobs but also environmental damage. There are several ways to manage moments of truth like these.

First, step back from traditional calculations such as cost-benefit analysis and ROI. Develop a habit of searching for the moral issues and ethical implications at stake in a given decision and analyze them using multiple philosophical perspectives. For instance, from the rule-based perspective of deontology (the study of moral obligation), ask yourself what rules or principles are relevant. Will a certain course of action lead you to violate the principle of being honest or of respecting others? From the consequence-based perspective of utilitarianism, identify potential outcomes for all parties involved or affected either directly or indirectly. What is the greatest good for the greatest number of people? And from the Aristotelian perspective of virtue ethics, ask yourself, Which course of action would best reflect a virtuous person? Each of these philosophies has advantages and disadvantages, but addressing the fundamental decision criteria of all three—rules, consequences, and virtues—will make you less likely to overlook important ethical considerations.

Note, however, that the human mind is skilled at justifying morally questionable behavior when enticed by its benefits. We often tell ourselves things such as "Everyone does this," "I'm just following my boss's orders," "It's for the greater good," "It's not like I'm robbing a bank," and "It's their own fault—they deserve it." Three tests can help you avoid self-deceptive rationalizations.

1. *The publicity test.* Would you be comfortable having this choice, and your reasoning behind it, published on the front page of the local newspaper?

2. *The generalizability test.* Would you be comfortable having your decision serve as a precedent for all people facing a similar situation?

3. *The mirror test.* Would you like the person you saw in the mirror after making this decision—is that the person you truly want to be?

If the answer to any of these questions is no, think carefully before proceeding.

Studies also show that people are more likely to act unethically if they feel rushed. Very few decisions must be made in the moment. Taking some time for contemplation can help put things in perspective. In a classic social psychology experiment, students at Princeton Theological Seminary were much less likely to stop and help a stranger lying helpless on the ground if they were rushing to get to a lecture they were scheduled to give—on, ironically, the biblical parable of the Good Samaritan, which is about stopping to help a stranger lying helpless on the ground. So be aware of time pressures. Minding the old adage "Sleep on it" can often help you make better moral decisions. And delaying a decision may give you time to consult your ethical mentors. If they are unavailable, practice a variation on the mirror and publicity tests: Imagine explaining your actions to those advisers. If that would make you uncomfortable, be warned.

But taking an ethical stand often requires challenging coworkers or even superiors, which can be excruciatingly difficult. The now infamous Milgram experiments (wherein study participants administered potentially lethal shocks to innocent volunteers when they were instructed to do so by an experimenter) demonstrated how susceptible people can be to pressure from others—especially those in positions of power. How can you avoid succumbing to social pressure? The authors of *The Business Ethics Field Guide* offer a few questions to ask yourself in such situations: Do they have a right to request that I do this? Would others in the organization feel the same way I do about this? What are the requesters trying to accomplish? Could it be accomplished in a different way? Can I refuse to comply in a manner that helps them save face? In general, be wary of doing anything just because "everybody else is doing it" or your boss told you to. Take ownership of your actions.

And don't forget that many ethical challenges people face at work have previously been confronted by others. As a result, companies often develop specific guidelines, protocols, and value statements. If in doubt about a certain situation, try consulting the formal policies of your organization. Does it have an established code of ethics? If not, ask your ethical mentor for guidance. And if you're dealing with something you view as clearly unethical but fear reprisal from a superior, check to see whether your organization has an ombudsman program or a whistle-blowing hotline.

Reflecting After the Fact

Learning from experience is an iterative, lifelong pursuit: A lot of growth happens after decisions are made and actions taken. Ethical people aren't perfect, but when they make mistakes, they review and reflect on them so that they can do better in the future. Indeed, a wide array of research—in fields as diverse as psychology, computer science, nursing, and education—suggests that reflection is a critical first step in learning from past personal experiences. Reflecting on both successes and failures helps people avoid not only repeated transgressions but also "identity segmentation," wherein they compartmentalize their personal and professional lives and perhaps live by a very different moral code in each.

But self-reflection has limitations. Sometimes ethical lapses are obvious; other times the choice is ambiguous. What's more, people can be hemmed in by their own perspectives as well as by their personal histories and biases. That's why we should seek the counsel of people we trust. You can approach this as you would job performance feedback: by asking specific questions, avoiding defensiveness, and expressing gratitude.

Finally, you can engage in what Amy Wrzesniewski of Yale calls *job crafting*: shaping your work experiences by proactively adapting the tasks you undertake, your workplace relationships, and even how you perceive your job, such that work becomes more meaningful and helps you fulfill your potential. You can apply job crafting to your ethical career by making bottom-up changes to your work and the way you approach it that will help you be more virtuous. For example, in some of the earliest studies on job crafting, Wrzesniewski and colleagues found that many hospital housekeepers viewed their work in a way that made them feel like healers, not janitors. They didn't just clean rooms; they helped create a peaceful healing environment. One custodian used her smile and humor to help cancer patients relax and feel more comfortable. She looked for opportunities to interact with them, believing that she could be a momentary bright spot in the darkness of their ongoing chemotherapy. She crafted her job to help her develop and cultivate eulogy virtues such as love, compassion, kindness, and loyalty.

. . .

You may feel that it isn't all that difficult to be an ethical professional. As your parents may have told you, just do the right thing. But the evidence suggests that out in the real world it becomes increasingly difficult to remain on the moral high ground. So take control of your ethical career by cultivating moral humility, preparing for challenging situations, maintaining your calm in the moment, and reflecting on how well you've lived up to your values and aspirations.

Originally published in January–February 2020. Reprint R2001L

3

Learning to Learn

by Erika Andersen

O rganizations today are in constant flux. Industries are consolidating, new business models are emerging, new technologies are being developed, and consumer behaviors are evolving. For executives, the ever-increasing pace of change can be especially demanding. It forces them to understand and quickly respond to big shifts in the way companies operate and how work must get done. In the words of Arie de Geus, a business theorist, "The ability to learn faster than your competitors may be the only sustainable competitive advantage."

I'm not talking about relaxed armchair or even structured classroom learning. I'm talking about resisting the bias against doing new things, scanning the horizon for growth opportunities, and pushing yourself to acquire radically different capabilities—while still performing your job. That requires a willingness to experiment and become a novice again and again: an extremely discomforting notion for most of us.

Over decades of coaching and consulting to thousands of executives in a variety of industries, however, my colleagues and I have come across people who succeed at this kind of learning.

We've identified four attributes they have in spades: aspiration, self-awareness, curiosity, and vulnerability. They truly want to understand and master new skills; they see themselves very clearly; they constantly think of and ask good questions; and they tolerate their own mistakes as they move up the learning curve.

Of course, these things come more naturally to some people than to others. But, drawing on research in psychology and management as well as our work with clients, we have identified some fairly simple mental tools anyone can develop to boost all four attributes—even those that are often considered fixed (aspiration, curiosity, and vulnerability).

Aspiration

It's easy to see aspiration as either there or not: You want to learn a new skill or you don't; you have ambition and motivation or you lack them. But great learners can raise their aspiration level—and that's key, because everyone is guilty of sometimes resisting development that is critical to success.

Think about the last time your company adopted a new approach—overhauled a reporting system, replaced a CRM platform, revamped the supply chain. Were you eager to go along? I doubt it. Your initial response was probably to justify not learning. *(It will take too long. The old way works just fine for me. I bet it's just a flash in the pan.)* When confronted with new learning, this is often our first roadblock: We focus on the negative and unconsciously reinforce our lack of aspiration.

When we *do* want to learn something, we focus on the positive—what we'll gain from learning it—and envision a happy future in which we're reaping those rewards. That propels us into action.

Idea in Brief

The ever-increasing pace of change in today's organizations requires that executives understand and then quickly respond to constant shifts in how their businesses operate and how work must get done. That means you must resist your innate biases against doing new things in new ways, scan the horizon for growth opportunities, and push yourself to acquire drastically different capabilities—while still doing your existing job. To succeed, you must be willing to experiment and become a novice over and over again, which for most of us is an extremely discomforting proposition.

Over decades of work with managers, the author has found that people who do succeed at this kind of learning have four well-developed attributes: aspiration, self-awareness, curiosity, and vulnerability. They have a deep desire to understand and master new skills; they see themselves very clearly; they're constantly thinking of and asking good questions; and they tolerate their own mistakes as they move up the curve. Andersen has identified some fairly simple mental strategies that anyone can use to boost these attributes.

Researchers have found that shifting your focus from challenges to benefits is a good way to increase your aspiration to do initially unappealing things. For example, when Nicole Detling, a psychologist at the University of Utah, encouraged aerialists and speed skaters to picture themselves benefiting from a particular skill, they were much more motivated to practice it.

A few years ago I coached a CMO who was hesitant to learn about big data. Even though most of his peers were becoming converts, he'd convinced himself that he didn't have the time to get into it and that it wouldn't be that important to his industry. I finally realized that this was an aspiration problem and encouraged him to think of ways that getting up to speed on data-driven marketing could help him personally. He acknowledged that it would be useful to know more about how various segments of his customer base were responding to his team's online advertising and in-store marketing campaigns. I then invited him to imagine the situation he'd be in a year later if he was getting that data. He started to show some excitement, saying, "We would be testing different approaches simultaneously, both in-store and online; we'd have good, solid information about which ones were working and for whom; and we could save a lot of time and money by jettisoning the less effective approaches faster." I could almost feel his aspiration rising. Within a few months he'd hired a data analytics expert, made a point of learning from her on a daily basis, and begun to rethink key campaigns in light of his new perspective and skills.

Self-Awareness

Over the past decade or so, most leaders have grown familiar with the concept of self-awareness. They understand that they need to solicit feedback and recognize how others see them. But when it comes to the need for learning, our assessments of ourselves—what we know and don't know, skills we have and don't have—can still be woefully inaccurate. In one study conducted by David Dunning, a Cornell University psychologist, 94% of college professors reported that they were doing "above average work." Clearly, almost half were wrong—many extremely so—and their self-deception surely diminished any appetite for development. Only 6% of respondents saw themselves as having a lot to learn about being an effective teacher.

In my work I've found that the people who evaluate themselves most accurately start the process inside their own heads: They accept that their perspective is often biased or flawed and then strive for greater objectivity, which leaves them much more open to hearing and acting on others' opinions. The trick is to pay attention to how you talk to yourself about yourself and then question the validity of that "self-talk."

Let's say your boss has told you that your team isn't strong enough and that you need to get better at assessing and developing talent. Your initial reaction might be something like *What? She's wrong. My team is strong.* Most of us respond defensively to that sort of criticism. But as soon as you recognize what you're thinking, ask yourself, *Is that accurate? What facts do I have to support it?* In the process of reflection you may discover that you're wrong and your boss is right, or that the truth lies somewhere in between—you cover for some of your reports by doing things yourself, and one of them is inconsistent in meeting deadlines; however, two others are stars. Your inner voice is most useful when it reports the facts of a situation in this balanced way. It should serve as a "fair witness" so that you're open to seeing the areas in which you could improve and how to do so.

One CEO I know was convinced that he was a great manager and leader. He did have tremendous industry knowledge and great instincts about growing his business, and his board acknowledged those strengths. But he listened only to people who affirmed his view of himself and dismissed input about shortcomings; his team didn't feel engaged or inspired. When he finally started to question his assumptions *(Is everyone on my team focused and productive? If not, is there something I could be doing differently?)*, he became much more aware of his developmental needs and open to feedback. He realized that it wasn't enough to have strategic insights; he had to share them with his reports and invite discussion, and then set clear priorities—backed by quarterly team and individual goals, regular progress checks, and troubleshooting sessions.

Curiosity

Kids are relentless in their urge to learn and master. As John Medina writes in *Brain Rules*, "This need for explanation is so powerfully stitched into their experience that some scientists describe it as a drive, just as hunger and thirst and sex are drives." Curiosity is what makes us try something until we can do it, or think about something until we understand it. Great learners retain this childhood drive, or regain it through another application of self-talk. Instead of focusing on and reinforcing initial disinterest in a new subject, they learn to ask themselves "curious questions" about it and follow those questions up with actions. Carol Sansone, a psychology researcher, has found, for example, that people can increase their willingness to tackle necessary tasks by thinking about how they could do the work differently to make it more interesting. In other words, they change their self-talk from *This is boring* to *I wonder if I could . . . ?*

You can employ the same strategy in your working life by noticing the language you use in thinking about things that already interest you—*How . . . ? Why . . . ? I wonder . . . ?*—and drawing on it when you need to become curious. Then take just one step to answer a question you've asked yourself: Read an article, query an expert, find a teacher, join a group—whatever feels easiest.

I recently worked with a corporate lawyer whose firm had offered her a bigger job that required knowledge of employment law—an area she regarded as "the single most boring aspect of the legal profession." Rather than trying to persuade her otherwise, I asked her what she was curious about and why. "Swing dancing," she said. "I'm fascinated by the history of it. I wonder how it developed, and whether it was a response to the

Changing your inner narrative

Unsupportive self-talk	Supportive self-talk
I don't need to learn this.	What would my future look like if I did?
I'm already fine at this.	Am I really? How do I compare with my peers?
This is boring.	I wonder why others find it interesting?
I'm terrible at this.	I'm making beginner mistakes, but I'll get better.

Depression—it's such a happy art form. I watch great dancers and think about why they do certain things."

I explained that her "curious language" could be applied to employment law. "I wonder how anyone could find it interesting?" she said jokingly. I told her that was actually an OK place to start. She began thinking out loud about possible answers ("Maybe some lawyers see it as a way to protect both their employees and their companies . . .") and then proposed a few other curious questions ("How might knowing more about this make me a better lawyer?").

Soon she was intrigued enough to connect with a colleague who was experienced in employment law. She asked him what he found interesting about it and how he had acquired his knowledge, and his answers prompted other questions. Over the following months she learned what she needed to know for that aspect of her new role.

The next time you're asked to learn something at the office, or sense that you should because colleagues are doing so, encourage yourself to ask and answer a few curious questions about it— *Why are others so excited about this? How might this make my job easier?*—and then seek out the answers. You'll need to find just one thing about a "boring" topic that sparks your curiosity.

Vulnerability

Once we become good or even excellent at some things, we rarely want to go back to being *not* good at other things. Yes, we're now taught to embrace experimentation and "fast failure" at work. But we're also taught to play to our strengths. So the idea of being bad at something for weeks or months; feeling awkward and slow; having to ask "dumb," "I-don't-know-what-you're-talking-about" questions; and needing step-by-step guidance again and again is extremely scary. Great learners allow themselves to be vulnerable enough to accept that beginner state. In fact, they become reasonably comfortable in it—by managing their self-talk.

Generally, when we're trying something new and doing badly at it, we think terrible thoughts: *I hate this. I'm such an idiot. I'll never get this right. This is so frustrating!* That static in our brains leaves little bandwidth for learning. The ideal mindset for a beginner is both vulnerable and balanced: *I'm going to be bad at this to start with, because I've never done it before. AND I know I can learn to do it over time.* In fact, the researchers Robert Wood and Albert Bandura found in the late 1980s that when people are encouraged to expect mistakes and learn from them early in the process of acquiring new skills, the result is "heightened interest, persistence, and better performance."

I know a senior sales manager from the United States who was recently tapped to run the Asia-Pacific region for his company. He was having a hard time acclimating to living overseas and working with colleagues from other cultures, and he responded by leaning on his sales expertise rather than acknowledging his beginner status in the new environment. I helped him recognize his resistance to being a cultural novice, and he was able to shift his self-talk from *This is so uncomfortable—I'll just focus on what*

I already know to *I have a lot to learn about Asian cultures. I'm a quick study, so I'll be able to pick it up.* He told me it was an immediate relief: Simply acknowledging his novice status made him feel less foolish and more relaxed. He started asking the necessary questions, and soon he was seen as open, interested, and beginning to understand his new environment.

. . .

The ability to acquire new skills and knowledge quickly and continually is crucial to success in a world of rapid change. If you don't currently have the aspiration, self-awareness, curiosity, and vulnerability to be an effective learner, these simple tools can help you get there.

Originally published in March 2016. Reprint R1603J

You Need Many Leadership Voices—Not Just One

by Amy Jen Su

We often equate developing a leadership voice with finding ways to appear more confident. We assume that our success depends upon mimicking someone else, increasing our self-promotion, or saying things louder than others. But rather than living with impostor syndrome or feeling exhausted by wearing your game face all day, you can build a truer confidence by more intentionally focusing on cultivating many different parts of your leadership voice each day. Ultimately, you should cultivate enough parts of your voice so that no matter what leadership situation or audience you are facing, you can respond in an authentic, constructive, and effective way. So, what are the various voices to access within yourself and cultivate over time? And what are the situations that warrant each one?

Your voice of character. First and foremost, consider the voice of your character. This is the part of you that is constant and consistent. It is grounded in fundamental principles about whom you choose to be and what guides and motivates your interactions with others. I've had leaders share that they hold key leadership principles in mind such as "Give the benefit of the doubt," "Don't take things personally," "Focus on what's best for the business," or "Be direct with respect" when walking into a difficult conversation, meeting, or conflict. Anchoring ourselves in the character we know we have keeps us from becoming chameleons, acting out of a fight-or-flight reaction, or showing respect only when there is a commercial gain or benefit—while being uncivil to others who we believe hold less value. A voice of character is ultimately about who you are and the intentions and motivations that guide your speech and actions.

Your voice of context. As you take on increasingly senior roles, your perspective of the business grows. You hold more of the big picture. Part of the job then becomes finding ways to express and communicate that bigger picture to others. Too often, in the race against time, we dive right into the details of a presentation, meeting, or conversation without taking an extra few minutes to appropriately set the stage and share critical context. Places where you can bring more of your voice of context include:

- Sharing your vision, strategy, or upcoming organizational change with others

- Presenting to executives and being clear on why you are there and what you need

- Kicking off a meeting with your team and giving the bigger picture for the topic at hand

Idea in Brief

The Challenge

Different situations require different approaches to leadership, so relying on a single style can limit your effectiveness.

The Solution

Leaders should cultivate a range of styles, from authoritative to empathetic, and learn when to apply each. Doing so takes self-awareness, emotional intelligence, and a willingness to continuously learn and grow. It also requires seeking feedback and being open to change.

The Payoff

Leaders who master multiple leadership voices can navigate complex situations more effectively, achieve better outcomes, and build stronger, more resilient teams.

- Clarifying your decision-making criteria or rationale for others

Your voice of clarity. In a world of high-intensity workplaces, you have the opportunity to be the voice of clarity and help your team stay focused on the most important priorities. Leaders who envision new possibilities, muse out loud, or have knee-jerk reactions run the risk of teams trying to deliver on their every whim; these teams end up scattered, spread thin, and unfocused, falling short on delivering on the most important wins. Here are a few ways you can be the voice of clarity to help channel others' energies more productively:

- At the start of the year, sit down with each direct report to prioritize and clarify what the big wins are in each of their areas. One client of mine shared how she asks each team member: "If we were to publish this in a newspaper, what would you want the big headlines to be for you and your team at the end of the year?"

- Periodically come back to helping your direct reports reprioritize what's on their plates. You can do this in one-on-one meetings or with your entire team.

- Empower your team to say no.

Your voice of curiosity. As a leader, you have a responsibility to give direction, share information, and make important decisions. But you need to be sure that you're not approaching every situation as if you have all the answers or need to advise on, problem-solve, or fix everything in front of you. In many cases, being the voice of curiosity is a better choice for the situation. As one of my clients once shared about facing pushback from others, "While I'm confident in my own business judgment and instincts, I know that my organization has hired really smart people. Therefore, if one of my peers or team members has a different perspective or pushes back, I don't take it personally. I get really curious to understand where they are coming from first so that we can get to the best solution." Some situations where bringing your voice of curiosity can help you and your colleagues move forward:

- You're engaging in work that is interdependent, and a better solution will come from hearing all perspectives in the room before coming to a final decision.

- You're coaching a direct report, and asking good questions to help them grow in new ways, explore issues they're facing, or support their career development.

- You're in a difficult conversation where hearing out the other person is an important part of diffusing emotion, understanding each party's needs and views, and then figuring out the best way forward.

Your voice of connection. As your span of control or influence grows, making a connection with a broadening set of colleagues, strategic networks, and teams can become increasingly difficult. We often have folks working for us many layers deep into the organization, such that we no longer know everyone in our area and still must find ways to stay connected and visible. Being a voice of connection can come in many forms. Some of the ways I've seen others do this effectively:

- Increase your skill as a storyteller. Stories make our points more memorable and salient. They can enliven a keynote address or an all-hands meeting, drive home a point we're making in a presentation, or help close a large deal or transaction.

- Thank and acknowledge. Our teams and colleagues often go to great lengths to ensure that deliverables are met, revenues are strong, and customers are satisfied. When we use our voice of connection, we express gratitude to a team that worked through the holidays to close on the financials at the end of the quarter, or loop back with a colleague who made a valuable introduction or referral for us.

- Make time for a few minutes of ice-breaking or rapport-building at the start of a conversation or meeting. So often, we want to get right down to business, so we skip the niceties or pleasantries that help build relationships with others. Where possible, and especially with colleagues who value that kind of connection, spend a couple of minutes to connect before diving in to the work. On days where you're crunched for time, state that up front and transparently so as not to create any misunderstandings. You can say something like: "I'm a little crunched for time today, so it would be great if we could dive right in."

Discovering and developing your voice as a leader is the work of a lifetime. The key is to stay open to an increasingly wide array of new situations and people. Use each situation as an opportunity to access more parts of your voice rather than having a one-size-fits-all approach. Bring your voices of character, context, clarity, curiosity, and connection as the moment or situation warrants. Through this kind of learning and growth, not only will you increase your inner confidence and resilience, but you will also inspire the confidence of others around you in a more authentic and impactful way.

Adapted from hbr.org, January 10, 2018. Reprint H043HT

4

Manage Your Energy, Not Your Time

by Tony Schwartz and Catherine McCarthy

Steve Wanner is a highly respected 37-year-old partner at Ernst & Young, married with four young children. When we met him a year ago, he was working 12- to 14-hour days, felt perpetually exhausted, and found it difficult to fully engage with his family in the evenings, which left him feeling guilty and dissatisfied. He slept poorly, made no time to exercise, and seldom ate healthy meals, instead grabbing a bite to eat on the run or while working at his desk.

Wanner's experience is not uncommon. Most of us respond to rising demands in the workplace by putting in longer hours, which inevitably take a toll on us physically, mentally, and emotionally. That leads to declining levels of engagement, increasing levels of distraction, high turnover rates, and soaring medical costs among employees. We at the Energy Project have worked with thousands of leaders and managers in the course of doing consulting and coaching at large organizations during the past five years. With remarkable consistency, these executives tell us they're pushing themselves harder than ever to keep up and increasingly feel they are at a breaking point.

The core problem with working longer hours is that time is a finite resource. Energy is a different story. Defined in physics as the capacity to work, energy comes from four main wellsprings in human beings: the body, emotions, mind, and spirit. In each, energy can be systematically expanded and regularly renewed by establishing specific rituals—behaviors that are intentionally practiced and precisely scheduled, with the goal of making them unconscious and automatic as quickly as possible.

To effectively reenergize their workforces, organizations need to shift their emphasis from getting more out of people to investing more in them, so they are motivated—and able—to bring more of themselves to work every day. To recharge themselves, individuals need to recognize the costs of energy-depleting behaviors and then take responsibility for changing them, regardless of the circumstances they're facing.

The rituals and behaviors Wanner established to better manage his energy transformed his life. He set an earlier bedtime and gave up drinking, which had disrupted his sleep. As a consequence, when he woke up he felt more rested and more motivated to exercise, which he now does almost every morning. In less than two months he lost 15 pounds. After working out he now sits down with his family for breakfast. Wanner still puts in long hours on the job, but he renews himself regularly along the way. He leaves his desk for lunch and usually takes a morning and an afternoon walk outside. When he arrives at home in the evening, he's more relaxed and better able to connect with his wife and children.

Idea in Brief

Organizations are demanding ever-higher performance from their workforces. People are trying to comply, but the usual method—putting in longer hours—has backfired. They're getting exhausted, disengaged, and sick. And they're defecting to healthier job environments.

Longer days at the office don't work because time is a limited resource. But personal energy is renewable, say Schwartz and McCarthy. By fostering deceptively simple rituals that help employees regularly replenish their energy, organizations build workers' physical, emotional, and mental resilience. These rituals include taking brief breaks at specific intervals, expressing appreciation to others, reducing interruptions, and spending more time on activities people do best and enjoy most.

Help your employees systematically rejuvenate their personal energy, and the benefits go straight to your bottom line. Take Wachovia Bank: Participants in an energy renewal program produced 13 percentage points greater year-over-year in revenues from loans than a control group did. And they exceeded the control group's gains in revenues from deposits by 20 percentage points.

Establishing simple rituals like these can lead to striking results across organizations. At Wachovia Bank, we took a group of employees through a pilot energy management program and then measured their performance against that of a control group. The participants outperformed the controls on a series of financial metrics, such as the value of loans they generated. They also reported substantial improvements in their customer relationships, their engagement with work, and their personal satisfaction. In this article, we'll describe the Wachovia study in a little more detail. Then we'll explain what executives and managers can do to increase and regularly renew work capacity—the approach used by the Energy Project, which builds on, deepens, and extends several core concepts developed by Tony's former partner Jim Loehr in his seminal work with athletes.

Linking Capacity and Performance at Wachovia

Most large organizations invest in developing employees' skills, knowledge, and competence. Very few help build and sustain their capacity—their energy—which is typically taken for granted. In fact, greater capacity makes it possible to get more done in less time at a higher level of engagement and with more sustainability. Our experience at Wachovia bore this out.

In early 2006 we took 106 employees at 12 regional banks in southern New Jersey through a curriculum of four modules, each of which focused on specific strategies for strengthening one of the four main dimensions of energy. We delivered it at one-month intervals to groups of approximately 20 to 25, ranging from senior leaders to lower-level managers. We also assigned each attendee a fellow employee as a source of support between sessions. Using Wachovia's own key performance metrics, we evaluated how the participant group performed compared with a group of employees at similar levels at a nearby set of Wachovia banks who did not go through the training. To create a credible basis for comparison, we looked at year-over-year percentage changes in performance across several metrics.

On a measure called the "Big 3"—revenues from three kinds of loans—the participants showed a year-over-year increase that was 13 percentage points greater than the control group's in the first three months of our study. On revenues from deposits, the participants exceeded the control group's year-over-year gain by 20 percentage points during that same period. The precise gains varied month by month, but with only a handful of exceptions, the participants continued to significantly outperform the control group for a full year after completing the program. Although other variables undoubtedly influenced these

How energy renewal programs boosted productivity at Wachovia

At Wachovia Bank, employees participating in an energy renewal program outperformed a control group of employees, demonstrating significantly greater improvements in year-over-year performance during the first quarter of 2006.

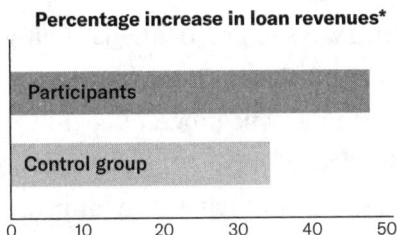

Percentage increase in loan revenues*

Participants

Control group

0 10 20 30 40 50

*From three critical kinds of loans

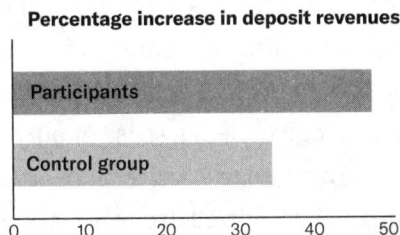

Percentage increase in deposit revenues

Participants

Control group

0 10 20 30 40 50

outcomes, the participants' superior performance was notable in its consistency.

We also asked participants how the program influenced them personally. Sixty-eight percent reported that it had a positive impact on their relationships with clients and customers. Seventy-one percent said that it had a noticeable or substantial positive impact on their productivity and performance. These findings corroborated a raft of anecdotal evidence we've gathered about the effectiveness of this approach among leaders at other large companies such as Ernst & Young (E&Y), Sony, Deutsche Bank, Nokia, ING Direct, Ford, and MasterCard.

The Body: Physical Energy

Our program begins by focusing on physical energy. It is scarcely news that inadequate nutrition, exercise, sleep, and rest diminish people's basic energy levels, as well as their ability to manage their emotions and focus their attention. Nonetheless, many executives don't find ways to practice consistently healthy behaviors, given all the other demands in their lives.

Before participants in our program begin to explore ways to increase their physical energy, they take an energy audit, which includes four questions in each energy dimension—body, emotions, mind, and spirit. On average, participants get eight to 10 of those 16 questions "wrong," meaning they're doing things such as skipping breakfast, failing to express appreciation to others, struggling to focus on one thing at a time, or spending too little time on activities that give them a sense of purpose. While most participants aren't surprised to learn these behaviors are counterproductive, having them all listed in one place is often uncomfortable, sobering, and galvanizing. The audit highlights employees' greatest energy deficits. Participants also fill out charts designed to raise their awareness about how their exercise, diet, and sleep practices influence their energy levels.

The next step is to identify rituals for building and renewing physical energy. When Gary Faro, a vice president at Wachovia, began the program, he was significantly overweight, ate poorly, lacked a regular exercise routine, worked long hours, and typically slept no more than five or six hours a night. That is not an unusual profile among the leaders and managers we see. Over the course of the program, Faro began regular cardiovascular and strength training. He started going to bed at a designated time and sleeping longer. He changed his eating habits from two big meals a day ("Where I usually gorged myself," he says) to smaller meals and light snacks every three hours. The aim was to help him stabilize his glucose levels over the course of the day, avoiding peaks and valleys. He lost 50 pounds in the process, and his energy levels soared. "I used to schedule tough projects for the morning, when I knew that I would be more focused," Faro says. "I don't have to do that anymore because I find that I'm just as focused now at 5 p.m. as I am at 8 a.m."

Another key ritual Faro adopted was to take brief but regular breaks at specific intervals throughout the workday—always leaving his desk. The value of such breaks is grounded in our physiology. "Ultradian rhythms" refer to 90- to 120-minute cycles during which our bodies slowly move from a high-energy state into a physiological trough. Toward the end of each cycle, the body begins to crave a period of recovery. The signals include physical restlessness, yawning, hunger, and difficulty concentrating, but many of us ignore them and keep working. The consequence is that our energy reservoir—our remaining capacity—burns down as the day wears on.

Intermittent breaks for renewal, we have found, result in higher and more sustainable performance. The length of renewal is less important than the quality. It is possible to get a great deal of recovery in a short time—as little as several minutes—if it involves a ritual that allows you to disengage from work and truly change channels. That could range from getting up to talk to a colleague about something other than work, to listening to music on an iPod, to walking up and down stairs in an office building. While breaks are countercultural in most organizations and counterintuitive for many high achievers, their value is multifaceted.

Are You Headed for an Energy Crisis?

Please check the statements below that are true for you.

Body

- ☐ I don't regularly get at least seven to eight hours of sleep, and I often wake up feeling tired.

- ☐ I frequently skip breakfast, or I settle for something that isn't nutritious.

- ☐ I don't work out enough (meaning cardiovascular training at least three times a week and strength training at least once a week).

- ☐ I don't take regular breaks during the day to truly renew and recharge, or I often eat lunch at my desk, if I eat it at all.

Emotions

- ☐ I frequently find myself feeling irritable, impatient, or anxious at work, especially when work is demanding.

- ☐ I don't have enough time with my family and loved ones, and when I'm with them, I'm not always really with them.

- ☐ I have too little time for the activities that I most deeply enjoy.

- ☐ I don't stop frequently enough to express my appreciation to others or to savor my accomplishments and blessings.

Mind

- ☐ I have difficulty focusing on one thing at a time, and I am easily distracted during the day, especially by email.

- ☐ I spend much of my day reacting to immediate crises and demands rather than focusing on activities with longer-term value and high leverage.

- ☐ I don't take enough time for reflection, strategizing, and creative thinking.

☐ I work in the evenings or on weekends, and I almost never take an email-free vacation.

Spirit

☐ I don't spend enough time at work doing what I do best and enjoy most.

☐ There are significant gaps between what I say is most important to me in my life and how I actually allocate my time and energy.

☐ My decisions at work are more often influenced by external demands than by a strong, clear sense of my own purpose.

☐ I don't invest enough time and energy in making a positive difference to others or to the world.

How is your overall energy?

Total number of statements checked: ___

Guide to scores

0–3: Excellent energy management skills
4–6: Reasonable energy management skills
7–10: Significant energy management deficits
11–16: A full-fledged energy management crisis

What do you need to work on?

Number of checks in each category:
Body ___
Mind ___
Emotions ___
Spirit ___

Guide to category scores

0: Excellent energy management skills
1: Strong energy management skills
2: Significant deficits
3: Poor energy management skills
4: A full-fledged energy crisis

Matthew Lang is a managing director for Sony in South Africa. He adopted some of the same rituals that Faro did, including a 20-minute walk in the afternoons. Lang's walk not only gives him a mental and emotional breather and some exercise but also has become the time when he gets his best creative ideas. That's because when he walks he is not actively thinking, which allows the dominant left hemisphere of his brain to give way to the right hemisphere with its greater capacity to see the big picture and make imaginative leaps.

The Emotions: Quality of Energy

When people are able to take more control of their emotions, they can improve the quality of their energy, regardless of the external pressures they're facing. To do this, they first must become more aware of how they feel at various points during the workday and of the impact these emotions have on their effectiveness. Most people realize that they tend to perform best when they're feeling positive energy. What they find surprising is that they're not able to perform well or to lead effectively when they're feeling any other way.

Unfortunately, without intermittent recovery, we're not physiologically capable of sustaining highly positive emotions for long periods. Confronted with relentless demands and unexpected challenges, people tend to slip into negative emotions—the fight-or-flight mode—often multiple times in a day. They become irritable and impatient, or anxious and insecure. Such states of mind drain people's energy and cause friction in their relationships. Fight-or-flight emotions also make it impossible to think clearly, logically, and reflectively. When executives learn to recognize what kinds of events trigger their negative emotions, they gain greater capacity to take control of their reactions.

One simple but powerful ritual for defusing negative emotions is what we call "buying time." Deep abdominal breathing is one way to do that. Exhaling slowly for five or six seconds induces relaxation and recovery, and turns off the fight-or-flight response. When we began working with Fujio Nishida, president of Sony Europe, he had a habit of lighting up a cigarette each time something especially stressful occurred—at least two or three times a day. Otherwise, he didn't smoke. We taught him the breathing exercise as an alternative, and it worked immediately: Nishida found he no longer had the desire for a cigarette. It wasn't the smoking that had given him relief from the stress, we concluded, but the relaxation prompted by the deep inhalation and exhalation.

A powerful ritual that fuels positive emotions is expressing appreciation to others, a practice that seems to be as beneficial to the giver as to the receiver. It can take the form of a handwritten note, an email, a call, or a conversation—and the more detailed and specific, the higher the impact. As with all rituals, setting aside a particular time to do it vastly increases the chances of success. Ben Jenkins, vice chairman and president of the General Bank at Wachovia in Charlotte, North Carolina, built his appreciation ritual into time set aside for mentoring. He began scheduling lunches or dinners regularly with people who worked for him. Previously, the only sit-downs he'd had with his direct reports were to hear monthly reports on their numbers or to give them yearly performance reviews. Now, over meals, he makes it a priority to recognize their accomplishments and also to talk with them about their lives and their aspirations rather than their immediate work responsibilities.

Finally, people can cultivate positive emotions by learning to change the stories they tell themselves about the events in their lives. Often, people in conflict cast themselves in the role of victim, blaming others or external circumstances for their problems. Becoming aware of the difference between the facts in a given situation and the way we interpret those facts can be powerful in itself. It's been a revelation for many of the people we work with to discover they have a choice about how to view a given event and to recognize how powerfully the story they tell influences the emotions they feel. We teach them to tell the most hopeful and personally empowering story possible in any given situation, without denying or minimizing the facts.

The most effective way people can change a story is to view it through any of three new lenses, which are all alternatives to seeing the world from the victim perspective. With the *reverse lens*, for example, people ask themselves, "What would the other person in this conflict say and in what ways might that be true?" With the *long lens* they ask, "How will I most likely view this situation in six months?" With the *wide lens* they ask themselves, "Regardless of the outcome of this issue, how can I grow and learn from it?" Each of these lenses can help people intentionally cultivate more positive emotions.

Nicolas Babin, director of corporate communications for Sony Europe, was the point person for calls from reporters when Sony went through several recalls of its batteries in 2006. Over time he found his work increasingly exhausting and dispiriting. After practicing the lens exercises, he began finding ways to tell himself a more positive and empowering story about his role. "I realized," he explains, "that this was an opportunity for me to build stronger relationships with journalists by being accessible to them and to increase Sony's credibility by being straightforward and honest."

The Mind: Focus of Energy

Many executives view multitasking as a necessity in the face of all the demands they juggle, but it actually undermines productivity. Distractions are costly: A temporary shift in attention from one task to another—stopping to answer an email or take a phone call, for instance—increases the amount of time necessary to finish the primary task by as much as 25%, a phenomenon known as "switching time." It's far more efficient to fully focus for 90 to 120 minutes, take a true break, and then fully focus on the next activity. We refer to these work periods as "ultradian sprints."

Once people see how much they struggle to concentrate, they can create rituals to reduce the relentless interruptions that technology has introduced in their lives. We start out with an exercise that forces them to face the impact of daily distractions. They attempt to complete a complex task and are regularly interrupted—an experience that, people report, ends up feeling much like everyday life.

Dan Cluna, a vice president at Wachovia, designed two rituals to better focus his attention. The first one is to leave his desk and go into a conference room, away from phones and email, whenever he has a task that requires concentration. He now finishes reports in a third of the time they used to require. Cluna built his second ritual around meetings at branches with the financial specialists who report to him. Previously, he would answer his phone whenever it rang during these meetings. As a consequence, the meetings he scheduled for an hour often stretched to two, and he rarely gave anyone his full attention. Now Cluna lets his phone go to voice mail, so that he can focus completely on the person in front of him. He now answers the accumulated voice-mail messages when he has downtime between meetings.

E&Y's hard-charging Wanner used to answer email constantly throughout the day—whenever he heard a "ping." Then he created a ritual of checking his email just twice a day—at 10:15 a.m. and 2:30 p.m. Whereas previously he couldn't keep up with all his messages, he discovered he could clear his inbox each time he opened it—the reward of fully focusing his attention on email for 45 minutes at a time. Wanner has also reset the expectations of all the people he regularly communicates with by email. "I've told them if it's an emergency and they need an instant response, they can call me and I'll always pick up," he says. Nine months later he has yet to receive such a call.

Michael Henke, a senior manager at E&Y, sat his team down at the start of the busy season last winter and told them that at certain points during the day he was going to turn off his Sametime (an in-house instant-message system). The result, he said, was that he would be less available to them for questions. Like Wanner, he told his team to call him if any emergency arose, but they rarely did. He also encouraged the group to take regular breaks throughout the day and to eat more regularly. They finished the busy season under budget and more profitable than other teams that hadn't followed the energy renewal program. "We got the same amount of work done in less time," says Henke. "It made for a win-win."

Another way to mobilize mental energy is to focus systematically on activities that have the most long-term leverage. Unless people intentionally schedule time for more challenging work, they tend not to get to it at all or rush through it at the last minute. Perhaps the most effective focus ritual the executives we work with have adopted is to identify each night the most important challenge for the next day and make it their very first priority when they arrive in the morning. Jean Luc Duquesne, a vice president for Sony Europe in Paris, used to answer his email as soon as he got to the office, just as many people do. He now tries to concentrate the first hour of every day on the most important topic. He finds that he often emerges at 10 a.m. feeling as if he's already had a productive day.

The Human Spirit: Energy of Meaning and Purpose

People tap into the energy of the human spirit when their everyday work and activities are consistent with what they value most and with what gives them a sense of meaning and purpose. If the work they're doing really matters to them, they typically feel more positive energy, focus better, and demonstrate greater perseverance. Regrettably, the high demands and fast pace of corporate life don't leave much time to pay attention to these issues, and many people don't even recognize meaning and purpose as potential sources of energy. Indeed, if we tried to begin our program by focusing on the human spirit, it would likely have minimal impact. Only when participants have experienced the value of the rituals they establish in the other dimensions do they start to see that being attentive to their own deeper needs dramatically influences their effectiveness and satisfaction at work.

For E&Y partner Jonathan Ansbacher, simply having the opportunity to ask himself a series of questions about what really mattered to him was both illuminating and energizing. "I think it's important to be a little introspective and say, 'What do you want to be remembered for?'" he told us. "You don't want to be remembered as the crazy partner who worked these long hours and had his people be miserable. When my kids call me and ask,

'Can you come to my band concert?' I want to say, 'Yes, I'll be there and I'll be in the front row.' I don't want to be the father that comes in and sits in the back and is on his Blackberry and has to step out to take a phone call."

To access the energy of the human spirit, people need to clarify priorities and establish accompanying rituals in three categories: doing what they do best and enjoy most at work; consciously allocating time and energy to the areas of their lives—work, family, health, service to others—they deem most important; and living their core values in their daily behaviors.

When you're attempting to discover what you do best and what you enjoy most, it's important to realize that these two things aren't necessarily mutually inclusive. You may get lots of positive feedback about something you're very good at but not truly enjoy it. Conversely, you can love doing something but have no gift for it, so that achieving success requires much more energy than it makes sense to invest.

To help program participants discover their areas of strength, we ask them to recall at least two work experiences in the past several months during which they found themselves in their "sweet spot"—feeling effective, effortlessly absorbed, inspired, and fulfilled. Then we have them deconstruct those experiences to understand precisely what energized them so positively and what specific talents they were drawing on. If leading strategy feels like a sweet spot, for example, is it being in charge that's most invigorating or participating in a creative endeavor? Or is it using a skill that comes to you easily and so feels good to exercise? Finally, we have people establish a ritual that will encourage them to do more of exactly that kind of activity at work.

A senior leader we worked with realized that one of the activities he least liked was reading and summarizing detailed sales reports, whereas one of his favorites was brainstorming new strategies. The leader found a direct report who loved immersing himself in numbers and delegated the sales report task to him—happily settling for brief oral summaries from him each day. The leader also began scheduling a free-form 90-minute strategy session every other week with the most creative people in his group.

In the second category, devoting time and energy to what's important to you, there is often a similar divide between what people say is important and what they actually do. Rituals can help close this gap. When Jean Luc Duquesne, the Sony Europe vice president, thought hard about his personal priorities, he realized that spending time with his family was what mattered most to him, but it often got squeezed out of his day. So he instituted a ritual in which he switches off for at least three hours every evening when he gets home, so he can focus on his family. "I'm still not an expert on PlayStation," he told us, "but according to my youngest son, I'm learning and I'm a good student." Steve Wanner, who used to talk on the cell phone all the way to his front door on his commute home, has chosen a specific spot 20 minutes from his house where he ends whatever call he's on and puts away the phone. He spends the rest of his commute relaxing so that when he does arrive home, he's less preoccupied with work and more available to his wife and children.

The third category, practicing your core values in your everyday behavior, is a challenge for many as well. Most people are living at such a furious pace that they rarely stop to ask themselves what they stand for and who they want to be. As a consequence, they let external demands dictate their actions.

We don't suggest that people explicitly define their values, because the results are usually too predictable. Instead, we seek to uncover them, in part by asking questions that are inadvertently revealing, such as, "What are the qualities that you find most off-putting when you see them in others?" By describing what they can't stand, people unintentionally divulge what they stand for. If you are very offended by stinginess, for example, generosity is probably one of your key values. If you are especially put off by rudeness in others, it's likely that consideration is a high value for you. As in the other categories, establishing rituals can help bridge the gap between the values you aspire to and how you currently behave. If you discover that consideration is a key value, but you are perpetually late for meetings, the ritual might be to end the meetings you run five minutes earlier than usual and intentionally show up five minutes early for the meeting that follows.

Addressing these three categories helps people go a long way toward achieving a greater sense of alignment, satisfaction, and well-being in their lives on and off the job. Those feelings are a source of positive energy in their own right and reinforce people's desire to persist at rituals in other energy dimensions as well.

This new way of working takes hold only to the degree that organizations support their people in adopting new behaviors. We have learned, sometimes painfully, that not all executives and companies are prepared to embrace the notion that personal renewal for employees will lead to better and more sustainable performance. To succeed, renewal efforts need solid support and commitment from senior management, beginning with the key decision-maker.

At Wachovia, Susanne Svizeny, the president of the region in which we conducted our study, was the primary cheerleader for the program. She embraced the principles in her own life and made a series of personal changes, including a visible commitment to building more regular renewal rituals into her work life. Next, she took it upon herself to foster the excitement and commitment of her leadership team. Finally, she regularly reached out by email to all participants in the project to encourage them in their rituals and seek their feedback. It was clear to everyone that she took the work seriously. Her enthusiasm was infectious, and the results spoke for themselves.

At Sony Europe, several hundred leaders have embraced the principles of energy management. Over the next year, more than 2,000 of their direct reports will go through the energy renewal program. From Fujio Nishida on down, it has become increasingly culturally acceptable at Sony to take intermittent breaks, work out at midday, answer email only at designated times, and even ask colleagues who seem irritable or impatient what stories they're telling themselves.

Organizational support also entails shifts in policies, practices, and cultural messages. A number of firms we worked with have built "renewal rooms" where people can regularly go to relax and refuel. Others offer subsidized gym memberships. In some cases, leaders themselves gather groups of employees for midday workouts. One company instituted a no-meeting zone between 8 and 9 a.m. to ensure that people had at least one hour absolutely free of meetings. At several companies, including Sony, senior leaders collectively agreed to stop checking email during meetings as a way to make the meetings more focused and efficient.

One factor that can get in the way of success is a crisis mentality. The optimal candidates for energy renewal programs are organizations that are feeling enough pain to be eager for new solutions but not so much that they're completely overwhelmed.

At one organization where we had the active support of the CEO, the company was under intense pressure to grow rapidly, and the senior team couldn't tear themselves away from their focus on immediate survival—even though taking time out for renewal might have allowed them to be more productive at a more sustainable level.

By contrast, the group at Ernst & Young successfully went through the process at the height of tax season. With the permission of their leaders, they practiced defusing negative emotions by breathing or telling themselves different stories, and alternated highly focused periods of work with renewal breaks. Most people in the group reported that this busy season was the least stressful they'd ever experienced.

The implicit contract between organizations and their employees today is that each will try to get as much from the other as they can, as quickly as possible, and then move on without looking back. We believe that is mutually self-defeating. Both individuals and the organizations they work for end up depleted rather than enriched. Employees feel increasingly beleaguered and burned out. Organizations are forced to settle for employees who are less than fully engaged and to constantly hire and train new people to replace those who choose to leave. We envision a new and explicit contract that benefits all parties: Organizations invest in their people across all dimensions of their lives to help them build and sustain their value. Individuals respond by bringing all their multidimensional energy wholeheartedly to work every day. Both grow in value as a result.

Originally published in October 2017. Reprint R0710B

5

Outsmart Your Own Biases

by Jack B. Soll, Katherine L. Milkman, and John W. Payne

S uppose you're evaluating a job candidate to lead a new office in a different country. On paper this is by far the most qualified person you've seen. Her responses to your interview questions are flawless. She has impeccable social skills. Still, something doesn't feel right. You can't put your finger on what—you just have a sense. How do you decide whether to hire her?

You might trust your intuition, which has guided you well in the past, and send her on her way. That's what most executives say they'd do when we pose this scenario in our classes on managerial decision-making. The problem is, unless you occasionally go against your gut, you haven't put your intuition to the test. You can't really know it's helping you make good choices if you've never seen what happens when you ignore it.

It can be dangerous to rely too heavily on what experts call System 1 thinking—automatic judgments that stem from associations stored in memory—instead of logically working through the information that's available. No doubt, System 1 is critical to survival. It's what makes you swerve to avoid a car accident. But as the psychologist Daniel Kahneman has shown, it's also a common source of bias that can result in poor decision-making, because our intuitions frequently lead us astray. Other sources of bias involve flawed System 2 thinking—essentially, deliberate reasoning gone awry. Cognitive limitations or laziness, for example, might cause people to focus intently on the wrong things or fail to seek out relevant information.

We are all susceptible to such biases, especially when we're fatigued, stressed, or multitasking. Just think of a CEO who's negotiating a merger while also under pressure from lawyers to decide on a plant closing and from colleagues to manage layoffs. In situations like this, we're far from decision-ready—we're mentally, emotionally, and physically spent. We cope by relying even more heavily on intuitive, System 1 judgments and less on careful reasoning. Decision-making becomes faster and simpler, but quality often suffers.

One solution is to delegate and to fight bias at the organizational level, using choice architecture to modify the environment in which decisions are made. Much of the time, though, delegation isn't appropriate, and it's all on you, the manager, to decide. When that's the case, you can outsmart your own biases. You start by understanding where they're coming from: excessive reliance on intuition, defective reasoning, or both. In this article, we describe some of the most stubborn biases out there: tunnel vision about future scenarios, about objectives, and about options. But awareness alone isn't enough, as

Idea in Brief

The Problem

Cognitive biases muddy our decision-making. We rely too heavily on intuitive, automatic judgments, and even when we try to use reason, our logic is often lazy or flawed.

The Cause

Instead of exploring risks and uncertainties, we seek closure—it's much easier. This narrows our thinking about what could happen in the future, what our goals are, and how we might achieve them.

The Solution

By knowing which biases tend to trip us up and using certain tricks and tools to outsmart them, we can broaden our thinking and make better choices.

Kahneman, reflecting on his own experiences, has pointed out. So we also provide strategies for overcoming biases, gleaned from the latest research on the psychology of judgment and decision-making.

First, though, let's return to that candidate you're considering. Perhaps your misgivings aren't really about her but about bigger issues you haven't yet articulated. What if the business environment in the new region isn't as promising as forecast? What if employees have problems collaborating across borders or coordinating with the main office? Answers to such questions will shape decisions to scale back or manage continued growth, depending on how the future unfolds. So you should think through contingencies now, when deciding whom to hire.

But asking those bigger, tougher questions does not come naturally. We're cognitive misers—we don't like to spend our mental energy entertaining uncertainties. It's easier to seek closure, so we do. This hems in our thinking, leading us to focus on *one possible future* (in this case, an office that performs as projected), *one objective* (hiring someone who can manage it under those circumstances), and *one option in isolation* (the candidate in front of us). When this narrow thinking weaves a compelling story, System 1 kicks in: Intuition tells us, prematurely, that we're ready to decide, and we venture forth with great, unfounded confidence. To "debias" our decisions, it's essential to broaden our perspective on all three fronts.

Thinking About the Future

Nearly everyone thinks too narrowly about possible outcomes. Some people make one best guess and stop there ("If we build this factory, we will sell 100,000 more cars a year"). Others at least try to hedge their bets ("There is an 80% chance we will sell between 90,000 and 110,000 more cars").

Unfortunately, most hedging is woefully inadequate. When researchers asked hundreds of chief financial officers from a variety of industries to forecast yearly returns for the S&P 500 over a nine-year horizon, their 80% ranges were right only one-third of the time. That's a terribly low rate of accuracy for a group of executives with presumably vast knowledge of the U.S. economy. Projections are even further off the mark when people assess their own plans, partly because their desire to succeed skews their interpretation of the data. (As former Goldman Sachs CFO David Viniar once put it, "The lesson you always learn is that your definition of extreme is not extreme enough.")

Because most of us tend to be highly overconfident in our estimates, it's important to "nudge" ourselves to allow for risk and uncertainty. The following methods are especially useful.

Make three estimates

What will be the price of crude oil in January 2017? How many new homes will be built in the United States next year? How many memory chips will your customers order next month? Such forecasts shape decisions about whether to enter a new market, how many people to hire, and how many units to produce. To improve your accuracy, work up at least three estimates—low, medium, and high—instead of just stating a range. People give wider ranges when they think about their low and high estimates separately, and coming up with three numbers prompts you to do that.

Your low and high guesses should be unlikely but still within the realm of possibility. For example, on the low end, you might say, "There's a 10% chance that we'll sell fewer than 10,000 memory chips next month." And on the high end, you might foresee a 10% chance that sales will exceed 50,000. With this approach, you're less likely to get blindsided by events at either extreme—and you can plan for them. (How will you ramp up production if demand is much higher than anticipated? If it's lower, how will you deal with excess inventory and keep the cash flowing?) Chances are, your middle estimate will bring you closer to reality than a two-number range would.

Think twice

A related exercise is to make two forecasts and take the average. For instance, participants in one study made their best guesses about dates in history, such as the year the cotton gin was invented. Then, asked to assume that their first answer was wrong, they guessed again. Although one guess was generally no closer than the other, people could harness the "wisdom of the inner crowd" by averaging their guesses; this strategy was more accurate than relying on either estimate alone. Research also shows that when people think more than once about a problem, they often come at it with a different perspective, adding valuable information. So tap your own inner crowd and allow time for reconsideration: Project an outcome, take a break (sleep on it if you can), and then come back and project another. Don't refer to your previous estimate—you'll only anchor yourself and limit your ability to achieve new insights. If you can't avoid thinking about your previous estimate, then assume it was wrong and consider reasons that support a different guess.

Use premortems

In a postmortem, the task is typically to understand the cause of a past failure. In a *premortem,* you imagine a future failure and then explain the cause. This technique, also called prospective hindsight, helps you identify potential problems that ordinary foresight won't bring to mind. If you're a manager at an international retailer, you might say: "Let's assume it's 2025, and our Chinese outlets have lost money every year since 2015. Why has that happened?"

Thinking in this way has several benefits. First, it tempers optimism, encouraging a more realistic assessment of risk. Second, it helps you prepare backup plans and exit strategies. Third, it can highlight factors that will influence success or failure, which may increase your ability to control the results.

Perhaps Home Depot would have benefited from a premortem before deciding to enter China. By some accounts, the company was forced to close up shop there because it learned too late that China isn't a do-it-yourself market. Apparently, given how cheap labor is, middle-class Chinese consumers prefer to contract out their repairs. Imagining low demand in advance might have led to additional market research (asking Chinese consumers how they solve their home-repair problems) and a shift from do-it-yourself products to services.

Take an outside view

Now let's say you're in charge of a new-product development team. You've carefully devised a six-month plan—about which you are very confident—for initial design, consumer testing, and prototyping. And you've carefully worked out what you'll need to manage the team optimally and why you expect to succeed. This is what Dan Lovallo and Daniel Kahneman call taking an "inside view" of the project, which typically results in excessive optimism. You need to complement this perspective with an outside view—one that considers what's happened with similar ventures and what advice you'd give someone else if you weren't involved in the endeavor. Analysis might show, for instance, that only 30% of new products in your industry have turned a profit within five years. Would you advise a colleague or a friend to accept a 70% chance of failure? If not, don't proceed unless you've got evidence that your chances of success are substantially better than everyone else's.

An outside view also prevents the "planning fallacy"—spinning a narrative of total success and managing for that, even though your odds of failure are actually pretty high. If you take a cold, hard look at the costs and the time required to develop new products in your market, you might see that they far outstrip your optimistic forecast, which in turn might lead you to change or scrap your plan.

Thinking About Objectives

It's important to have an expansive mindset about your objectives, too. This will help you focus when it's time to pick your most suitable options. Most people unwittingly limit themselves by allowing only a subset of worthy goals to guide them, simply because they're unaware of the full range of possibilities.

That's a trap the senior management team at Seagate Technology sought to avoid in the early 1990s, when the company was the world's largest manufacturer of disk drives. After acquiring a number of firms, Seagate approached the decision analyst Ralph Keeney for help in figuring out how to integrate them into a single organization. Keeney conducted individual interviews with 12 of Seagate's top executives, including the CEO, to elicit the firm's goals. By synthesizing their responses, he identified eight general objectives (such as creating the best software organization and providing value to customers) and 39 specific ones (such as developing better product standards and reducing customer costs). Tellingly, each executive named, on average, only about a third of the specific objectives, and only one person cited more than half. But with all the objectives mapped out, senior managers had a more comprehensive view and a shared framework for deciding which opportunities to pursue. If they hadn't systematically reflected on their goals, some of those prospects might have gone undetected.

Early in the decision-making process, you want to generate many objectives. Later you can sort out which ones matter most. Seagate, for example, placed a high priority on improving products because that would lead to more satisfied customers, more sales, and ultimately greater profits. Of course, there are other paths to greater profits, such as developing a leaner, more efficient workforce. Articulating, documenting, and organizing your goals helps you see those paths clearly so that you can choose the one that makes the most sense in light of probable outcomes. Take these steps to ensure that you're reaching high—and far—enough with your objectives.

Seek advice

Round out your perspective by looking to others for ideas. In one study, researchers asked MBA students to list all their objectives for an internship. Most mentioned seven or eight things, such as "improve my attractiveness for full-time job offers" and "develop my leadership skills." Then they were shown a master list of everyone's objectives and asked which ones they considered personally relevant. Their own lists doubled in size as a result—and when participants ranked their goals afterward, those generated by others scored as high as those they had come up with themselves.

Outline objectives on your own before seeking advice so that you don't get "anchored" by what others say. And don't anchor your advisers by leading with what you already believe ("I think our new CFO needs to have experience with acquisitions—what do you think?"). If you are making a decision jointly with others, have people list their goals independently and then combine the lists, as Keeney did at Seagate.

Cycle through your objectives

Drawing on his consulting work and lab experiments, Keeney has found that looking at objectives one by one rather than all at once helps people come up with more alternatives. Seeking a solution that checks off every single box is too difficult—it paralyzes the decision-maker.

So, when considering your goals for, say, an off-site retreat, tackle one at a time. If you want people to exchange lessons from the past year, develop certain leadership skills, and deepen their understanding of strategic priorities, thinking about these aims separately can help you achieve them more effectively. You might envision multiple sessions or even different events, from having expert facilitators lead brainstorming sessions to attending a leadership seminar at a top business school. Next, move on to combinations of objectives. To develop leadership skills and entertain accompanying family members, you might consider an Outward Bound–type experience. Even if you don't initially like an idea, write it down—it may spark additional ideas that satisfy even more objectives.

Thinking About Options

Although you need a critical mass of options to make sound decisions, you also need to find strong contenders—at least two but ideally three to five. Of course, it's easy to give in to the tug of System 1 thinking and generate a false choice to rationalize your intuitively favorite option (like a parent who asks an energetic toddler, "Would you like one nap or two today?"). But then you're just duping yourself. A decision can be no better than the best option under consideration. Even System 2 thinking is often too narrow. Analyzing the pros and cons of several options won't do you any good if you've failed to identify the best ones.

Unfortunately, people rarely consider more than one at a time. Managers tend to frame decisions as yes-or-no questions instead of generating alternatives. They might ask, for instance, "Should we expand our retail furniture business into Brazil?" without questioning whether expansion is even a good idea and whether Brazil is the best place to go.

Yes-no framing is just one way we narrow our options. Others include focusing on one type of solution to a problem (what psychologists call functional fixedness) and being constrained by our assumptions about what works and what doesn't. All these are signs of cognitive rigidity, which gets amplified when we feel threatened by time pressure, negative emotions, exhaustion, and other stressors. We devote mental energy to figuring out how to avoid a loss rather than developing new possibilities to explore.

Use joint evaluation

The problem with evaluating options in isolation is that you can't ensure the best outcomes. Take this scenario from a well-known study: A company is looking for a software engineer to write programs in a new computer language. There are two applicants, recent graduates of the same esteemed university. One has written 70 programs in the new language and has a 3.0 (out of 5.0) grade point average. The other has written 10 programs and has a 4.9 GPA. Who gets the higher offer?

The answer will probably depend on whether you look at both candidates side by side or just one. In the study, most people who considered the two programmers at the same time—in joint evaluation mode—wanted to pay more money to the more prolific recruit, despite his lower GPA. However, when other groups of people were asked about only one programmer each, proposed salaries were higher for the one with the better GPA. It is hard to know whether 70 programs is a lot or a little when you have no point of comparison. In separate evaluation mode, people pay attention to what they can easily evaluate—in this case, academic success—and ignore what they can't. They make a decision without considering all the relevant facts.

A proven way to snap into joint evaluation mode is to consider what you'll be missing if you make a certain choice. That forces you to search for other possibilities. In a study at Yale, 75% of respondents said yes when asked, "Would you buy a copy of an entertaining movie for $14.99?" But only 55% said yes when explicitly told they could either buy the movie or keep the money for other purchases. That simple shift to joint evaluation highlights what economists call the opportunity cost—what you give up when you pursue something else.

Try the "vanishing options" test

Once people have a solid option, they usually want to move on, so they fail to explore alternatives that may be superior. To address this problem, the decision experts Chip Heath and Dan Heath recommend a mental trick: Assume you can't choose any of the options you're weighing and ask, "What else could I do?" This question will trigger an exploration of alternatives. You could use it to open up your thinking about expanding your furniture business to Brazil: "What if we *couldn't* invest in South America? What else could we do with our resources?" That might prompt you to consider investing in another region instead, making improvements in your current location, or giving the online store a major upgrade. If more than one idea looked promising, you might split the difference: for instance, test the waters in Brazil by leasing stores instead of building them, and use the surplus for improvements at home.

Fighting Motivated Bias

All these cognitive biases—narrow thinking about the future, about objectives, and about options—are said to be "motivated" when driven by an intense psychological need, such as a strong emotional attachment or investment. Motivated biases are especially difficult to overcome. You know this if you've ever poured countless hours and resources into developing an idea, only to discover months later that someone has beaten you to it. You should move on, but your desire to avoid a loss is so great that it distorts your perception of benefits and risks. And so you feel an overwhelming urge to forge ahead—to prove that your idea is somehow bigger or better.

Our misguided faith in our own judgment makes matters worse. We're overconfident for two reasons: We give the information we do have too much weight (see the sidebar "How to Prevent Misweighting"). And because we don't know what we can't see, we have trouble imagining other ways of framing the problem or working toward a solution.

But we can preempt some motivated biases, such as the tendency to doggedly pursue a course of action we desperately want to take, by using a "trip wire" to redirect ourselves to a more logical path. That's what many expedition guides do when leading clients up Mount Everest: They announce a deadline in advance. If the group fails to reach the summit by then, it must head back to camp—and depending on weather conditions, it may have to give up on the expedition entirely. From a rational perspective, the months of training and preparation amount to sunk costs and should be disregarded. When removed from the situation, nearly everyone would agree that ignoring the turnaround time

How to Prevent Misweighting

When we assign too much or too little significance to the information we have, we're bound to go off course in our decision making. It's a problem that cuts across the different types of bias, but here are some tactics that can help.

Utility	Examples
Blinding: Improves judgment by eliminating the influence of stereotypes, idiosyncratic associations, and irrelevant factors.	Orchestras have players audition behind a screen to prevent gender bias. After this became standard practice, female membership skyrocketed from 5% in 1970 to nearly 40% today.
	Many professors ensure fair grading by covering up names (or asking an assistant to do so) before evaluating papers and other assignments.
Checklists: Reduce errors due to forgetfulness and other memory distortions by directing our attention to what's most relevant.	Venture capitalists often use a set list of criteria to vet entrepreneurial pitches.
	Savvy hiring managers assess candidates by conducting structured interviews (they're much more accurate predictors of performance than open-ended interviews). Because there's a standard way to rate responses, people can be easily compared on various dimensions.

Algorithms: Ensure consistency by predetermining how much emphasis each piece of information will get.[a]

Banks and other lenders use scoring algorithms to predict consumers' credit-worthiness.

Taking a page from professional baseball, employers are starting to use algorithms in hiring. One study showed that a simple equation for evaluating applicants outperformed human judgment by at least 25%.

a. Since algorithms reflect the biases of the experts who build them, it's best to combine them with other debiasing tools.

would put lives at stake and be too risky. However, loss aversion is a powerful psychological force. Without a trip wire, many climbers do push ahead, unwilling to give up their dream of conquering the mountain. Their tendency to act on emotion is even stronger because System 2 thinking is incapacitated by low oxygen levels at high altitudes. As they climb higher, they become less decision-ready—and in greater need of a trip wire.

In business, trip wires can make people less vulnerable to "present bias"—the tendency to focus on immediate preferences and ignore long-term aims and consequences. For instance, if you publicly say *when* you'll seek the coaching that your boss wants you to get (and that you've been putting off even though you know it's good for you), you'll be more apt to follow through. Make your trip wire precise (name a date) so that you'll find it harder to disregard later, and share it with people who will hold you accountable.

Another important use of trip wires is in competitive bidding situations, where the time and effort already invested in a negotiation may feel like a loss if no deal is reached. Executives often try to avoid that loss by escalating their commitment, overpaying by millions or even billions of dollars. The thing is, preferences often change over the course of a negotiation (for example, new information that comes to light may justify paying a higher price). So in this sort of situation, consider setting a *decision point*—a kind of trip wire that's less binding because it triggers thinking instead of a certain action. If the deal price escalates beyond your trigger value, take a break and reassess your objectives and options. Decision points provide greater flexibility than "hard" trip wires, but because they allow for multiple courses of action, they also increase your risk of making short-term, emotion-based decisions.

Although narrow thinking can plague us at any time, we're especially susceptible to it when faced with one-off decisions, because we can't learn from experience. So tactics that broaden our perspective on possible futures, objectives, and options are particularly valuable in these situations. Some tools, such as checklists and algorithms, can improve decision readiness by reducing the burden on our memory or attention; others, such as trip wires, ensure our focus on a critical event when it happens.

As a rule of thumb, it's good to anticipate three possible futures, establish three key objectives, and generate three viable options for each decision scenario. We can always do more, of course, but this general approach will keep us from feeling overwhelmed by endless possibilities—which can be every bit as debilitating as seeing too few.

Even the smartest people exhibit biases in their judgments and choices. It's foolhardy to think we can overcome them through sheer will. But we *can* anticipate and outsmart them by nudging ourselves in the right direction when it's time to make a call.

Originally published in May 2015. Reprint R1505D

6

Happiness Traps

by Annie McKee

L
ife is too short to be unhappy at work. Yet many professionals who are free to shape their careers are just that: disengaged, unfulfilled, and miserable. Take Sharon, a vice
president at a global energy firm and one of my consulting
clients. She's smart and hardworking and has risen through the
ranks by following the rules. She makes a lot of money, is married
to a man she loves, and is devoted to her children. She had everything she thought she wanted, but she wasn't happy. Things
were tense at home, and work no longer gratified her. She was
tired of workplace politics and cynical about the never-ending
changes that would supposedly fix whatever was wrong with the
company in a given quarter. She resented the long hours she was
required to put in. That next promotion and bonus weren't as
enticing as they used to be, but she still worked as hard as ever:
Striving was a habit.

Sharon blamed others for her disenchantment. She believed
that the executive team was disconnected from the day-to-day
business. She complained to friends and coworkers about management's bad decisions, the company's strategy, and what she

perceived as a lack of vision on the part of senior leadership. All the members of her team seemed to be slacking.

After coaching Sharon for several months, I grew to like her. But even I found her complaints tedious. I can only imagine what her coworkers thought. When we finally got past why everyone else was to blame for her dissatisfaction, she said, "I know I could probably make things better. I'm just so busy. Besides, it doesn't matter whether I'm happy or not. What matters is that I hit my targets." In her more reflective moments, Sharon admitted that her stress and unhappiness were affecting her work relationships, her family, and her health. She even noticed that she had begun to compromise her ethics in small ways. What she didn't see was the link between her growing misery and her dwindling ability to do her job effectively.

Sharon is not alone. For years we've heard about dismal levels of employee engagement. Numerous studies show that close to two-thirds of employees in the United States are bored, detached, or jaded and ready to sabotage plans, projects, and other people. This makes no sense to me. Why do so many of us accept unsatisfying work, high levels of stress, looming burnout, and chronic unhappiness? Why don't we fight back?

Multiple factors account for this contemporary malaise. The American Psychological Association found early in 2017 that Americans are reporting more stress than ever owing to politics, the speed of change, and uncertainty in the world. But it's not always outside forces that push us over the happiness line. Sometimes we do it to ourselves. Throughout my 30-year career advising leaders of major businesses, governments, and NGOs around the globe, I've discovered that far too many of us fall into common "happiness traps"—destructive mindsets and ways of working that keep us stuck, unhappy, and ultimately less successful.

Idea in Brief

The Conundrum

Why are so many of us who can shape our professional lives unhappy at work? And what can we do about it?

The Traps

We often fall into destructive mindsets and ways of working that make us unsatisfied and ultimately less successful. Some of the most common of these "happiness traps"—ambition (win at all costs); doing what's expected rather than what we want; and overwork—seem productive on the surface but are harmful when taken to the extreme.

The Path Forward

Finding happiness at work begins with honing your emotional intelligence to grasp which trap has ensnared you. Then you can foster three things that are known to increase professional satisfaction: meaningful work, enduring hope, and workplace friendships.

Three of the most common happiness traps—ambition, doing what's expected of us, and working too hard—seem productive on the surface but are harmful when taken to the extreme.

The Ambition Trap

The drive to achieve goals and further our careers pushes us to be and do our best. But when ambition is coupled with hyper-competitiveness and a single-minded focus on winning, we get into trouble. We become blind to the impact of our actions on ourselves and others; relationships are damaged and collaboration suffers; we start chasing goals for the sake of hitting targets; and work begins to lose its meaning.

That's exactly what happened to Sharon. Throughout her life, her parents, teachers, and coaches encouraged her striving, and she attained a lot. She got good grades, top spots on sports teams, and academic awards. When she started working, her ambition impressed her bosses: She gave them what they wanted on time and well done.

Her peers weren't quite as enthralled, however, and some steered clear as they realized that Sharon always wanted to be number one. To her, that meant everyone else had to be number two. Team goals were not a priority unless they served her purpose, and she got a reputation for throwing people under the bus.

Nothing is inherently wrong with ambition, of course. Sometimes it leads people to hone social skills; after all, effective collaboration is a prerequisite for long-term success in complex organizations. But Sharon's unfettered ambition was focused solely on her own goals, and peers soon stopped trusting her. They also stopped helping her.

Sharon's workplace challenges came to a head while she was managing a highly visible project, serving as the interface between her division and a powerful internal client. The company's strategy shifted, project goals changed, and the client's standards were raised, although funding remained flat. Sharon repeatedly heard the client's requests as unreasonable demands and responded as she often had—by turning the situation into a win-lose competition. She began to cut corners, demanded that her division be paid excessive amounts of money for the work it was doing, and even told a falsehood or two to get what she wanted.

Sharon's boss, who had protected her for years, finally had to admit the obvious: She had become a liability. He removed her from the project and sidelined her. Her career stalled. Being forced off the fast track was a wake-up call, and Sharon came to see that she had been lonely and deeply unhappy at work for a very long time. Her ambition had turned into a trap instead of an asset. Her ruthlessness was a learned behavior rather than an inherent quality: Success early on had reinforced a winner-take-all attitude that ultimately derailed her both professionally and personally.

The "Should" Trap

Doing what we think we should do rather than what we want to do is a trap that all of us risk falling into at some point in our work lives. True, some of the unwritten rules that shape our careers are positive, such as completing an education so that we can help our families and observing punctuality and civility at work. But too many of our workplace norms—what I call *shoulds*—force us to deny who we are and to make choices that hinder our potential and stifle our dreams.

To be successful in most companies, people have to obey shoulds about how to dress, how to talk, whom to associate with, and sometimes even how to have a life outside work. I've worked in organizations where a candidate's scuffed shoes kill his chances of getting the job and where women must wear makeup and have certain (usually short) hairstyles. I've also been in companies where it's impossible for men to rise to leadership roles unless they are married—to women. And at the *Fortune* 500 only 4% of senior leaders are female, and fewer than 1% are people of color. These shocking statistics tell a tale of who "should" lead and who "should" follow.

Such unspoken norms are not only unfounded (gender, race, and marital status have no correlation with leadership ability); they also take a personal toll when we feel we must hide who we are or pretend to be someone we're not. Kenji Yoshino and Christie

Smith showed in a Deloitte-sponsored study of more than 3,000 workers that 61% of people feel they have to "cover" in some way to fit in at work: They either actively hide or downplay their gender, race, sexual orientation, religion, or other aspects of their identities, personalities, or lives.

At some companies women don't talk about their children to avoid the "motherhood penalty." African Americans often avoid one another so as not to be seen as part of a marginalized group. Even 45% of white men report covering things that set them apart, such as depression or a child who struggles at school. I have known many who hide anything that makes them look weak or vulnerable—difficulties at home, feeling burned out— because they feel they should be strong all the time.

Shoulds don't just affect how we project ourselves at work. They often dictate what kind of job and career we aspire to. Take another of my coaching clients, Marcus. During his junior and senior years of college, Marcus was involved with a couple of startups, and he relished the experience. He secretly hoped to continue on the entrepreneurship track, but as graduation loomed, he found himself wavering. When he got an offer from a prestigious consultancy, he took the job. Six months in he realized that he hated it, but with parents still bragging about his big job and salary and envious friends asking him to get them into the company, he felt he couldn't quit.

At 42 Marcus was made a partner in the firm. He'd followed all the rules and, on the surface, was a true winner. But that's the problem: His career felt like a game. He saw a disconnect between the firm's mission and what it really did, yet he went along. He recognized that how he was expected to treat people— especially junior people—was dehumanizing, yet he did it.

Marcus didn't like consulting and had spent much of his career hiding who he really is: a gay man married to a union carpenter. He had never disclosed details about his personal life at work because it was clear that those who succeeded at his company were straight, and as far as he knew, no other spouses worked with their hands. Living in hiding makes anyone unhappy. And it drags down professional performance as commitment wanes and displeasure with work and colleagues eventually becomes obvious.

Avoiding the should trap isn't about completely ignoring the rules, of course. Absolute nonconformity and cultural deviance would challenge even the most inclusive organization. Instead, we need to recognize which rules end up being harmful. Self-suppression and diligent conformity don't bring out our most original, creative contributions at work; nor do they lead to workplace happiness, a key ingredient of sustained professional success. In this case the shoulds that directed his professional choices caused Marcus to take the wrong job and hide his personal life. The rules he thought he must obey became soul destroying and ultimately dragged down his career.

The Overwork Trap

Some of us react to the very real pressures of the "always on" 21st-century workplace by spending every waking moment working or thinking about work. We don't have time for friends, exercise, healthful food, or sleep. We don't play with our children or even listen to them. We don't stay home when we're sick. We don't take the time to get to know people at work or put ourselves in their shoes before we jump to conclusions.

Overwork sucks us into a negative spiral: More work causes more stress; increased stress causes our brains to slow down and compromises our emotional intelligence; less creativity and poor people skills harm our ability to get things done. As the title of a recent *Harvard Business Review* article nicely summarized, "The Research Is Clear: Long Hours Backfire for People and for Companies."

Overwork is seductive, because it is still lauded in so many workplaces. Boston University's Erin Reid found, in fact, that some people (men in particular) lie about how many hours they work. They claim to put in 80-plus-hour weeks—presumably because they think excessive hours impress their bosses. What's more, obsession with work can stem from our inner demons: It feeds on our insecurities, assuages our guilt when we see others overwork, or helps us escape personal troubles. Many overworkers believe that working more will alleviate stress: If they just finish that project, get that report done, read all that email, they'll feel less out of control. But of course the work never ends.

That happened to Marcus. He would come home in the evenings—usually later than he had promised—and spend time in the kitchen talking with his spouse and asking the kids about their day. All the while, his phone was sitting on the counter. Two minutes into the conversation he'd pick it up. He thought his family didn't care, but naturally they were hurt. Over the years, his spouse tried to talk about Marcus's preoccupation with work. At first Marcus would explode: "I have to do this! What do you want me to do, quit?" Eventually he'd be contrite and promise to change. But after a short remission, his addiction would return.

Marcus started sleeping less—in part because of late-night and early-morning calls, and in part from stress. He didn't eat well, and he found himself drinking too much. At work he was a grumpy, distracted boss. He began making mistakes—missing deadlines, forgetting to respond to critical emails. He couldn't live up to his own or others' expectations, which bothered him tremendously. So he just tried harder.

Like Sharon, Marcus finally got a wake-up call. His came at home. One evening, during their never-ending argument about the phone, the emails, and the calls at night, his spouse gave him an ultimatum: "This has to stop," he said. "I won't go on like this." That hit Marcus hard, and it came at a telling moment. The week before, his boss had pointed out some serious problems in one of his projects. She told him that everyone was worried about him—his switch was always "on," and it was obvious that he was burning out. She'd even said the same thing his spouse did: "This has to stop."

Marcus struggled to admit he had a problem. Overwork disguised as diligence was part of his identity—and, as is true for many of us, it seemed more important as his career progressed and the pace of change increased. Flatter, leaner companies and ultracompetitive markets force us to do more with less. As technology has advanced, we are performing tasks that others used to do—or do for us. For the many of us who work across time zones, early-morning and late-night conference calls are now routine. And that little device we carry everywhere is a demanding master. Work is literally in our pockets—or on our nightstands.

Whether you've fallen into the "shoulds" and the overwork traps, as Marcus did, or the ambition trap, as Sharon did, the question is, How can you get out? The good news is that some of the same leadership skills and mindsets that make you effective at work can help you escape and rediscover happiness there.

Breaking Free

The first step is to accept that you deserve happiness at work. That means giving up the misbelief that work is not meant to be a primary source of fulfillment. For centuries it was simply a means of staving off hunger. To be sure, many people still struggle with low wages and horrible working conditions, and for them, work may equal drudgery. But research has shown that even menial jobs can provide fulfillment. What's surprising is that successful executives—today's knowledge workers and creatives—sometimes don't find true meaning in their work. Instead they buy into the myth that it's a grind.

Work can be a source of real happiness, which I define as a deep and abiding enjoyment of daily activities fueled by passion for a meaningful purpose, a hopeful view of the future, and true friendships. To embrace these three components of happiness, we must first delve into the very personal drivers and habits that keep us from fostering them. Why do we work all the time? Do our ambition and desire to win serve us or hurt us? Why are we trapped by what we feel we *should* do and not pursuing what we *want* to do? To answer these questions, we need to tap into our emotional intelligence.

Moving from Trapped to Happy

Over the past several decades, psychologists and researchers, myself included, have come to agree that there are 12 emotional intelligence competencies, all of which can help you avoid or break free from the happiness traps. I believe that three—emotional self-awareness, emotional self-control, and organizational awareness—are particularly useful when casting off an outdated mindset.

The Emotional Intelligence Competencies

Self-Awareness
Emotional self-awareness

Social Awareness
Empathy
Organizational awareness

Self-Management
Positive outlook
Achievement orientation
Adaptability
Emotional self-control

Relationship Management
Inspirational leadership
Teamwork
Coach and mentor
Influence
Conflict management

Source: Annie McKee, Richard Boyatzis, and Frances Johnston, *Becoming a Resonant Leader* (Boston: Harvard Business Press, 2008).

Emotional self-awareness is the capacity to notice and understand your feelings and moods and to recognize how they affect your thoughts and actions. You might realize, for example, that the discomfort you feel when you buck a work "should"—such as replying to email at 8 p.m. or during the weekend—signals that you're afraid of being excluded. Going a bit deeper, you might see that this fear has little or nothing to do with your current work situation; it may simply be an old habit of mind that no longer serves you.

Awareness is a good start, but then you need to act. This is where emotional self-control comes in: It enables you to tolerate the discomfort that arises when you understand what you are doing to yourself. For instance, if you know that you check your email at night out of insecurity, you're not going to feel particularly good about yourself. But if you push that feeling aside, you will remain stuck. Self-control also enables us to take actions that may fall outside our comfort zone.

Finally, organizational awareness—an understanding of your work environment—can help you distinguish between what is coming from inside you and what's coming from others or your company. Say, for example, that you're aware that your colleagues are reading and sending emails at all hours and that your overwork comes from pressure to conform—not necessarily from insecurity. Now you see that you have a choice to make: You can bravely decide to buck the norms and quit overworking, or you can continue to behave in a way that conflicts with your values (and harms your health and family life). You might even recognize that pulling back from overworking could change the dynamics and expectations of your team, creating a virtuous microculture within the larger organization.

Purpose, Hope, and Friendship

Using emotional intelligence to remove barriers to happiness is a first step on the journey to greater fulfillment at work. But happiness doesn't happen magically—we must actively seek meaning and purpose in our day-to-day activities, foster hope in ourselves and others, and build friendships at work.

Meaning and purpose

Humans are wired to seek meaning in everything we do, whether we're sitting in an office, hiking in the mountains, or eating dinner with the family. Passion for a cause fuels energy, intelligence, and creativity. Brain chemistry is in part responsible: Researchers have shown that the positive emotions aroused by work we see as worthwhile enable us to be smarter, more innovative, and more adaptable. For example, the Duke psychology professor Dan Ariely and colleagues conducted a study in which participants were paid to build Lego models, some of which were dismantled in front of them upon completion. People whose creations were preserved made, on average, 50% more Lego models than those whose models were destroyed, despite identical monetary incentives. We give more of ourselves when we have an impact—even if it's a small one.

Management scholars have shown that the same holds true on the job: Purpose is a powerful driver of workplace happiness. Yet too often we fail to tap this wellspring of motivation. As was true for Sharon and Marcus, it's easy to lose sight of what we value and ignore the aspects of work that matter to us, especially if we struggle with dysfunctional organizations, bad bosses, and stress. And if that happens, disengagement is just around the corner. In the absence of meaning, we have no reason to give our all.

Each of us finds meaning and purpose in work differently, but in my experience with people from all over the globe and in all professions, I've seen some similarities: We want to fight for a cause we care about. We want to create and innovate. We want to fix problems and improve our workplaces. We want to learn and grow. And, as studies have shown, meaningful work is as possible and important for a janitor or a middle manager as it is for a CEO.

Breaking Free from Happiness Traps

Three common traps—ambition, "shoulds," and overwork—keep people from being happy and fulfilled in their careers. Courageously looking at the ones you've fallen into is the beginning of taking control. Start by asking yourself these questions:

- Which happiness traps keep me in my comfort zone or make me feel safe?

- Which traps keep me from pursuing my dreams for a better job, a great career, or real fulfillment in the job I have now?

- Which traps do I keep others in?

Next choose the happiness trap that most affects you.

- How does it help or hurt you?

- How does it affect your relationships? Other people may benefit (or think they do) when we are trapped, or they may be hurt. Who in your life benefits from the trap you're in? Who is harmed?

- Imagine a life without this happiness trap. What would it feel like? What would you do? How would others benefit if you were free from it? To bring this to life, write three paragraphs as if you were already in the future, starting with "It is now three years since I broke free. I feel . . . I am now . . . The people in my life are . . ."

As you discover which aspects of your job are truly fulfilling—and which are soul-destroying—you will face choices about how to spend your time and what to pursue in your career. Marcus decided to begin seriously exploring that business he'd always dreamed of having. He looked at finances and at how to leverage his relationships at his current firm and with clients. He and his spouse considered the lifestyle changes that launching a business would require. In the end, he created a bridge: He worked as an associate at his firm part-time for two years while seeking funding and starting his new business.

Hope

If you've ever faced adversity, a crisis, or a loss, you know that hope is what got you through. It makes us want to get up every day and keep trying, even when life is tough. Hope makes it possible to navigate complexity; handle stress, fear, and frustration; and understand hectic organizations and lives. That's in part because hope, like purpose, positively affects our brain chemistry. Research has shown that when we feel optimistic, our nervous system shifts from fight-or-flight to calm and poised to act. For example, one study demonstrated that when individuals are coached in a way that sparks positive feelings and an inspiring vision of the future, areas of the brain associated with the parasympathetic nervous system are activated: Breathing slows, blood pressure drops, and the immune system functions better. We think more rationally and are better able to manage our emotions. We feel energized and ready to plan for the future.

That's how Sharon moved from awareness of why she was so focused on winning to creating a career that she was authentically excited about. Through conversations with her husband (who had cautioned her for years about her unregulated ambition), she was able to craft a vision of what she wanted from her work—one that relied not on getting the next promotion or winning some endless game but on the kind of life she wanted to lead.

Employers often use vision statements to instill optimism and positivity in their employees, but unfortunately even the most well-crafted ones are rarely compelling enough to keep people hopeful over the long term. To be happy at work, we must feel that our responsibilities and opportunities fit a *personal* vision—one that speaks to our values, desires, and beliefs—and we must imagine pathways that lead to it. Hope is really about planning—it encourages us to chart a course even in the face of seemingly dire prospects; it encourages us to take concrete, practical actions that are tied to how we want our lives and careers to unfold.

I've met many people in my work who shy away from big dreams, fearing that they'll only be disappointed. But I don't believe there's any such thing as false hope. Hope is not magical thinking or fantasy; it's a powerful, positive emotional experience that leads to courage, thoughtful plans, and concrete actions.

Friendship

If you work with people you like and respect, and if they like and respect you in return, you probably enjoy going to work. But if you're in a job where you feel constantly on guard, disdained, or excluded, you're probably on your way to deep unhappiness—or there already. You may tell yourself that the situation is tolerable or that you don't need friends at work. That's not true.

In fact, good relationships are the backbone of successful organizations. People who care for one another give generously of time, talent, and resources. Gallup found that close work relationships boost employee satisfaction by 50% and that people with a best friend at work are seven times as likely as others to engage fully in their work. Mutual respect motivates us to resolve conflicts so that everyone wins. And when we believe that we will be accepted for who we are, that we have important roles to play, and that we're part of a team, we are more committed to collective goals.

Warm, positive relationships are important at work for very human reasons. Since the beginning of time, people have organized into tribes that labor and play together. Today organizations are our tribes. We want to work in a group or a company that makes us proud and inspires us to give our best efforts. We also want people to care about us and value us as human beings. And we need to do the same for others. We thrive physically and psychologically when we feel compassion for others and see that they are concerned for our well-being in return. In fact, the Harvard Grant Study, among others, has found that love—yes, love—is the single most important determinant of happiness in life. What's more, people who experience love—including the love involved in friendships—are more successful, even financially. (The study notes that during peak earning years, participants who scored highest on "warm relationships" made an average of $141,000 more a year.)

But love at work? Most people shy away from the notion, leery of romance in the workplace (although we know it occurs often). What we need at work, however, is love founded on caring, concern, and camaraderie. Such relationships are full of trust and generosity, a source of delight, and make work fun.

· · ·

Too many people believe that if they're successful, they'll be happy. That's backward. The author and psychologist Shawn Achor says it straightforwardly: "Happiness comes before success." That's because the positive emotions aroused by being engaged, fulfilled, and valued at work have a host of benefits: Our brains function better; we are more creative and adaptable; we have more energy, make smarter decisions, and better manage complexity. It's simple: Happy people perform better than their unhappy peers.

It's time to claim our right to happiness at work. To start, let's replace outdated beliefs with a new understanding of what we can expect from work—and from one another. Let's break free of traps that keep us from happiness. And let's begin the journey to fulfillment by focusing on discovering and living our purpose at work, reaching for a compelling vision of the future, and turning colleagues into real friends. These things will help us create workplaces that honor our humanity and foster common decency and sustainable success, workplaces in which ideas, needs, and desires matter—as does happiness.

Originally published in September–October 2017. Reprint R1705D

7

The Hidden Toll of Microstress

by Rob Cross and Karen Dillon

A few years ago, we interviewed a pharmaceuticals executive who seemed to have built an ideal life. She was excelling at work, her personal life was rich and full, and she was able to take regular vacations, whose destinations were chosen by virtue of where she and her husband could run marathons together. In our interview, she was happy and her energy was off the charts.

Her story was great to hear but perhaps not surprising—the interview was part of our research into what makes high performers different from the rest of us. She was, we thought, a case study in having it all. But as it turned out, we didn't know the full story. This interview also led us to discover something we weren't looking to find. Something bigger.

The executive hadn't always had such a balanced life. In fact, she'd only gotten herself together after a stern warning from her doctor, who said the way she'd been living was jeopardizing her physical health. Prior to being the high performer we interviewed, this woman was a self-described sedentary workaholic who was thriving in neither her personal nor her professional life. How had someone who was clearly goal-driven neglected her well-being so drastically? On a whim, we asked her what had thrown her off track in the first place. For a moment, she was stumped.

"It was just life, I guess."

The answer intrigued us, so we started asking other high performers if their lives were feeling out of control or had pushed them in directions not aligned with who they set out to be. In total we interviewed 300 people from 30 global companies, evenly split between women and men, from 2019 to 2021. Many of these high performers were powder kegs of stress, and to our surprise, most of them didn't realize it. But gradually, usually deep into our interview, they began to acknowledge that they were struggling to keep up with both work and their personal lives. For some, our interviews were an inflection point, the moment they first recognized just how bad things had gotten. Some even broke down into tears, lamenting that they couldn't see a path out of barely holding it together.

After decades of research on collaboration, and specifically the effects of too much ineffective collaboration, we were familiar with the kinds of stress that high performers typically endure. This, though, was completely different. What we were hearing about was stress, yes, but in a form that neither they—nor we—had the language to articulate. As they fumbled to describe it, patterns emerged. It was never one big thing that led them to feel overwhelmed. Rather, it was the relentless accumulation of unnoticed small events—in passing moments—that was drastically affecting their well-being.

Idea in Brief

Microstresses are small moments of stress that seem manageable on their own—think a vague, worrying text from your teen flashing on your phone while you're in a meeting, the appearance of a colleague who always wants to vent to you, or having to tell your team that the project you've all been grinding out extra hours on is no longer a priority. But these microstresses aren't as harmless as they seem. Because they're so small and brief, they don't trigger the normal stress response in our brains to help us cope; instead, microstress embeds itself in our minds and accrues over time. The long-term impact of this buildup is debilitating: It saps our energy, damages our physical and emotional health, and contributes to a decline in our overall well-being. But once you understand the science behind microstress and where it comes from, you can fight back. Fresh research will teach you how to recognize and manage microstress's most common forms.

We called these small pressures *microstresses*. But being "micro" doesn't mean they don't take an enormous toll in the long run. In this article we will describe how we came to understand microstress, where it comes from, and how our bodies respond to it. We have grouped the most common sources of microstress into three categories so that you can understand how they arise in your life. And finally, we'll explain how you can push back on microstress to feel more in control, strengthen your relationships, and improve your overall well-being.

Stress vs. Microstress

Microstress is different from the type of stress we're all familiar with. Here's how.

Stress is big, visible, and obvious. Virtually everyone can recognize, and have sympathy for, normal stress—it comes from universally recognized challenges or setbacks, and often there's a "bad guy" who is the source of it. Maybe it's caused by reporting to a mercurial boss whose daily mood permeates the entire office. Or by having survived multiple rounds of layoffs that eliminated positions in your department. Or by managing a house move, or continually being called on to help dependent parents, or enduring a grinding, two-hour commute.

By contrast, *microstress* is far less obvious. It's caused by difficult moments that we register as just another bump in the road—if we register them at all. Microstresses come at us so quickly, and we're so conditioned to just working through them, that we barely recognize anything has happened. They tend to seem fleeting, simple to deal with, or too minor to hurt us for more than a second. And even when we do register microstress, we don't necessarily think about its impact on our lives. Making it even harder to recognize is the fact that microstress is often triggered by the people we are closest to.

For example, it might be caused by feeling the need to protect an employee on your team who isn't getting recognized for their work. Or by having to put in extra time to finish a joint project when your teammates fall short on their part. Or by your manager's suddenly changing a project after you've called in favors to get it done, wasting your and your coworkers' time. Or even by knowing that you'll have to miss your weekly tennis game with a friend (again), making you feel that you've let them down once more and that your skills are declining.

Microstresses, as their name implies, are small—often invisible to us. Yet they also sometimes seem like positives or easy-to-justify decisions that, in the moment, appear harmless. After all, you're stepping up in some way to help others. How can it be bad to feel poorly for a minute about unintentionally wasting your friends' time? Why not pick up the slack for your lax coworker? It's only an extra 15 minutes of work for you that will help the whole team.

But that's exactly what is so pernicious about microstress. Individual stressors seem manageable in the moment, but they accrue, and they can create ripple effects of secondary and sometimes tertiary consequences that can last for hours or days—and even trigger microstress in others. For example, if your teammates fail to complete a key task, you'll have to clean up their underdelivery and have an uncomfortable conversation about what happened. In addition, you'll have to ask your partner to take your child to the dentist, even though it's your turn and the child likes that you always remember to pack their favorite toy. And beyond that, you might not have time to work on a professional development project as you'd planned to.

Microstresses may be hard to spot individually, but cumulatively they pack an enormous punch.

Microstress also involves emotional baggage that's not easy to unpack. That's because the source of microstress is seldom a classic antagonist, such as a spectacularly demanding client or a jerk boss. Rather, it comes from the people with whom we are closest: our friends, family members, and colleagues. For example, we may harbor feelings of guilt or failure that we've let down someone we care about, or find ourselves in situations where we're concerned for their well-being. If you're a manager responsible for a team of employees, you might worry constantly about whether you're mentoring them well enough, or whether you need to supervise them closely so that they don't screw up in front of colleagues. The emotion in the relationship—positive or negative—magnifies the impact of the stressor.

The ripple effect of microstress

One small, seemingly inconsequential moment can play out long beyond the original instant of microstress—sometimes even for days.

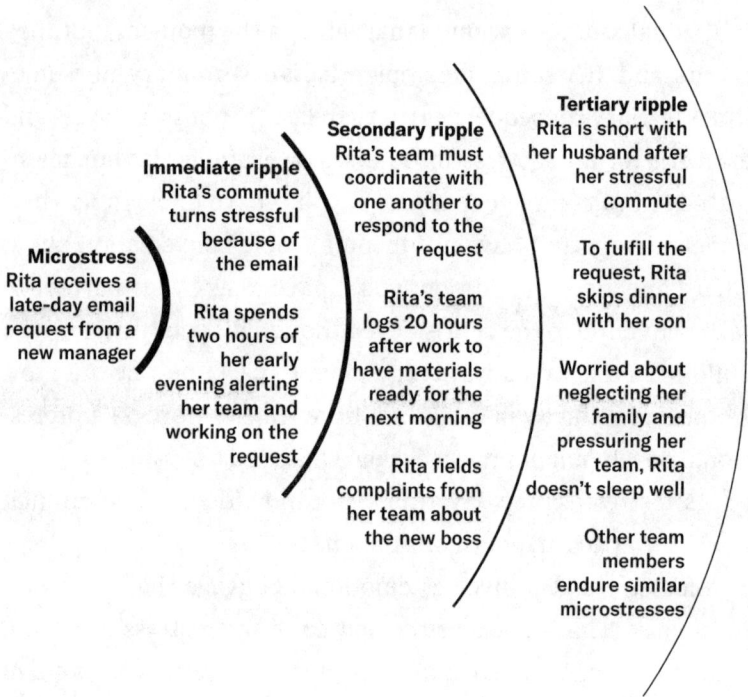

Microstress
Rita receives a late-day email request from a new manager

Immediate ripple
Rita's commute turns stressful because of the email

Rita spends two hours of her early evening alerting her team and working on the request

Secondary ripple
Rita's team must coordinate with one another to respond to the request

Rita's team logs 20 hours after work to have materials ready for the next morning

Rita fields complaints from her team about the new boss

Tertiary ripple
Rita is short with her husband after her stressful commute

To fulfill the request, Rita skips dinner with her son

Worried about neglecting her family and pressuring her team, Rita doesn't sleep well

Other team members endure similar microstresses

Of course, you're never coping with just one or two microstresses. You're likely facing dozens a day—and you've probably come to accept that this hectic way of living is nothing special. "Just let me survive this one week," you promise yourself, planning to get through any rough patches with a little bit of willpower. "Then I'll be OK." Unfortunately, too many of us have fallen into a reactive posture by accepting that we now live in a hyperconnected, 24/7 world, with everyone a simple text, call, or video chat away. As a result, we're on call around the clock; the interconnectedness of our work and home lives is staggering.

Except *every* week becomes yet another week you just have to survive—and the cycle continues for months on end. We find ourselves teetering on the edge of burnout almost all the time, and we can't quite put our finger on why.

There's a biological reason for that.

The Biology of Microstress

Microstress is pernicious because it is part of our everyday lives at a greater volume, intensity, and pace than we have ever experienced before, and that's only increasing with technology and ubiquitous connectivity. And our bodies don't quite know what to make of it.

The process by which we respond to normal stress is called *allostasis*, the biologic mechanism that protects the body from it. Allostasis helps us maintain internal homeostasis, or internal balance. Our brains know how to register conventional forms of stress, so they can identify the threat and use the extra oomph of the fight-or-flight mechanisms that kick in to deal with it.

But microstressors can fly under the radar of our fight-or-flight vigilance systems while still taking a significant toll, says Joel Salinas, a behavioral neurologist and researcher at the New York University Grossman School of Medicine and the chief medical officer at Isaac Health, which provides online brain-health services. "Imagine wind eroding a mountain," Salinas told us. "It's not the same as a big TNT explosion that punches a hole in a mountain, but over time—if the wind never stops—it has the potential to slowly whittle the entire mountain down to a nub."

We may not be consciously aware of microstressors, but like plain old stress they, too, can increase our blood pressure and our heart rate, or trigger hormonal or metabolic changes. "While microstressors are damaging our bodies, our brains are not fully registering them as a threat," Salinas explained. "Therefore, our brains are not triggering the same kind of protective higher-order mechanisms that might occur in the face of more obvious stress."

This dynamic is due in part to how the brain processes information. Our "working memory," which lives in the frontal lobe, is where we keep mental notes—it's a kind of mental "scratch pad," as Salinas puts it. But under continual stress, the scratch pad tends to shrink, making it harder to keep track of things that require our response or attention. That explains why so many of us felt "brain fog" during the pandemic, whether we had Covid-19 or not: Our brains were slowly taken up with microstressors, so the bandwidth we would typically have for paying attention to an activity or solving a problem was simply not available. Additionally, when the scratch pad shrinks, we literally may not remember why we're feeling out of sorts—which helps microstresses slip past our defenses. "This is arguably worse than threats that cross the fight-or-flight threshold," Salinas told us. "Not only are you not noticing [microstress], but it can also have more-severe consequences."

You may be quicker to dismiss microstress than more macro forms of stress because you think you can just manage it in the moment. The thing is, your brain *isn't* managing it, because your normal stress response didn't fire. So microstresses accrue, one on top of another.

In fact, the human brain doesn't seem to distinguish between different sources of chronic stress, according to neuroscientist

Lisa Feldman Barrett, a distinguished professor of psychology at Northeastern University and the author of *Seven and a Half Lessons About the Brain*. That's because our brains are constantly trying to coordinate all our systems—cardiovascular, respiratory, immune, endocrine, gastrointestinal, and others—in the most metabolically efficient way. The coordination is a brain-body transaction that we end up feeling as *mood* (which, Barrett explains, is a simple accounting of how you are feeling, such as comfortable, tired, or wired—and is distinct from emotions like sadness and happiness).

For the transaction, Barrett says, our brains do a "body budgeting" to assess the cumulative effect of the stressors we experience on a day-to-day basis. Importantly, while individual microstresses—say, a misalignment with your teammates at work—may feel small, "when they add together, they can have a massive impact," she says. "If your body budget is already depleted by the circumstances of life—like physical illness, financial hardship, hormone surges, or simply not sleeping or exercising enough—your brain becomes more vulnerable to stress of all kinds. You may end up feeling ground down into a pulp."

For example, Barrett continues, one study found that if you're exposed to social stress within two hours of a meal, your body metabolizes the food in a way that adds 104 calories to the meal. "If this happens daily, that's 11 pounds gained per year! Not only that, but if you eat healthful, unsaturated fats—such as those found in nuts—within one day of being stressed, your body metabolizes these foods as if they were filled with bad fats." Further, Barrett adds, in her research she has been able to stimulate a cortisol surge in test subjects by subtly implying, through her tone of voice or behavior, that they are being evaluated negatively (in effect, creating microstress). In our everyday lives, then, as we face the microstress of negative interactions with other people, our body budgets are being depleted even if we barely register the negativity in the moment. These momentary "withdrawals" add up.

"When your body budget is continually burdened, momentary stressors pile up, even the kind that you'd normally bounce back from quickly. It's like children jumping on a bed," says Barrett. "The bed might withstand 10 kids bouncing at the same time, but the 11th one snaps the bed frame."

The Sources and Effects of Microstress

Where is all this microstress that we hardly notice coming from?

Our research has identified 14 sources, in three broad categories:

Microstresses that drain your capacity to get things done. These are why so many of us feel that we're failing at work and in our personal lives: We can barely get through our daily responsibilities. The sources are:

- Misalignment between collaborators on their roles or priorities

- Uncertainty about others' reliability

- Unpredictable behavior from a person in a position of authority

- Collaborative demands that are diverse and high in volume

- Surges in responsibilities at work or home

Microstresses that deplete your emotional reserves. These are disruptions to the internal "well" of peace, fortitude, and resilience that helps you focus, prioritize, and manage conflict. The sources are:

- Managing and feeling responsible for the success and well-being of others

- Confrontational conversations

- Lack of trust in your network

- People who spread stress

- Political maneuvering

Microstresses that challenge your identity. These trigger the uncomfortable feeling that you're not the person you really want to be, which can chip away at your motivation and sense of purpose. The sources are:

- Pressure to pursue goals out of sync with your personal values

- Attacks on your sense of self-confidence, worth, or control

- Draining or otherwise negative interactions with family or friends

- Disruptions to your network

Most of us experience several of these microstresses in our day-to-day lives. For example, as the director of the Interdisciplinary Affective Science Laboratory at Northeastern, Barrett may understand the toll microstress takes on her brain, but that doesn't make her immune to it. "When I'm overwhelmed by the number of things I have to do, and someone else's outcomes are depending on my doing something, my husband will say, 'Well, that's the mark of a successful person,'" she says. "And maybe that's true, but it only goes so far. I run a lab of 25 young scientists, and every single one of those people depends on me for something. I have an impact on their outcomes. We don't just make deposits and withdrawals in our own body budgets. We are also the caretakers of other people's body budgets."

For example, Kunal, a senior leader in the automotive industry, shared the frustration he felt when he had to redo the work of a subordinate who turned in a substandard product. "It creates a sort of seething bitterness and stress, because I'm now spending time on something I shouldn't have to," he told us. "Doing their work displaces other things and contributes to an environment where I don't have the energy and time to develop my team." Beyond redoing the project, Kunal also had to find time to address the performance issue—which added a whole other layer of microstress to his day. "That requires extra energy because you have to be understanding and then follow almost a Socratic process that walks someone through the preparation they should have done."

And those were just the immediate consequences. Over time the situation built resentment, caused Kunal to call in favors from other team members, and meant that he often brought his frustration home at night. He was aware that he was doing it, but he couldn't seem to shake off the day.

Kunal's story is merely one example of the toll of one employee's falling just a bit short. Multiply the consequences by the endless interactions we have—whether we find ourselves misaligned with coworkers, juggling ever-increasing responsibilities, or even feeling uncomfortable with our boss's request to use high-pressure sales tactics on customers. For most of us, every day is a minefield of microstresses.

Making matters more complicated is the fact that one of the primary sources of microstress is the people we are closest to. Marriage, for instance, is one of the most salient sources of support—but can also be a trigger for microstress. Consider the ripple effects when we exchange curt words with our spouses about some inconsequential chore or task before work, then spend all day thinking about the interaction. Once we get home that night, all may be forgiven, but the worrying has already impacted our day in ways that don't disappear quickly. We may be distracted at work, leading us to perform worse or let our colleagues down, which will almost surely ricochet back at us.

Fighting Microstress

So, what can we do about the battering of microstress in our daily lives? Conventional advice for improving our well-being tends to focus on steeling yourself against stress (macro or micro), such as through mindfulness, meditation, or gratitude. Yes, these approaches help refresh your mind. But in a way, they also hurt, as they build your ability to *endure* more microstress.

Wouldn't it be better if you were able to remove some of the microstress in your life instead? From decades of social science research, we know that a negative interaction is up to *five times* more impactful than a positive one. That means finding ways to eliminate even just a few microstresses in your life can make a significant difference. Our research suggests that most people can find three to five obvious opportunities to make a notable difference in their microstress level, using three strategies:

- *Push back on microstress in concrete, practical ways.* You can find small but effective ways to counter microstressors that will have an outsize impact in your daily life. These range from learning how to say no to small asks, to managing technology and how it notifies and interrupts you, to readjusting relationships to prevent others from putting microstress on you.

- *Be attuned to the microstress you are causing others.* This won't just help them—it will help you too. When we create microstress for others, it inevitably boomerangs in one form or another. (A simple example is when microstress causes you to snap at your partner, which inevitably leads to anger or resentment that swings back on you.) Emitting less means we'll receive less in return.

- *Rise above.* One reason some microstressors affect us is simply because we allow them to. You can learn to keep some of them in perspective and let things that bother you just roll off your back. This is not a call to be a Pollyanna—we found that the happiest people in our research were able to put some of the microstress in their lives in perspective. In part, that was because they tended to belong to two or three groups in their lives—outside of their professions—that were meaningful to them. The dimensionality these activities and groups brought to their lives served a very real purpose of helping them recognize when minutiae was minutiae. In contrast, those people who allowed their lives to become too unidimensional often swam in a sea of microstress that they helped create. And they couldn't rise above any of it.

What's Driving Your Microstress?

Microstresses infiltrate our lives in ways we often don't realize. Here are the 14 types of microstress, broken down into three categories. Which resonate with your daily experiences?

Microstresses That Drain Your Capacity to Get Things Done

- Misalignment between collaborators on their roles or priorities
- Uncertainty about others' reliability
- Unpredictable behavior from a person in a position of authority
- Collaborative demands that are diverse and high in volume
- Surges in responsibilities at work or home

Microstresses That Deplete Your Emotional Reserves

- Managing and feeling responsible for the success and well-being of others
- Confrontational conversations
- Lack of trust in your network
- People who spread stress
- Political maneuvering

Microstresses That Challenge Your Identity

- Pressure to pursue goals out of sync with your personal values
- Attacks on your sense of self-confidence, worth, or control
- Draining or otherwise negative interactions with family or friends
- Disruptions to your network

That is, of course, just a quick summary of the approaches our most successful interviewees used to keep microstress in check. Reducing the microstress in your life requires identifying where it's coming from (recognizing that the sources may not be obvious), tracking and understanding the ripple effects, and devising effective ways to push back. What it *doesn't* require is overhauling your life.

To kick off the process, use the list of the 14 microstress sources from earlier in the chapter to help you identify which ones have the greatest impact on your life. It will also help you discover where you might be causing microstress for others and which stresses you think you can rise above. The diagnostic contains a glossary that goes into additional detail about each source.

The Power of Other People

One of the most interesting insights from our research was that, while people are the cause of the microstress in your life, they're part of the solution too. As neuroscientist Barrett explains, the worst thing for your nervous system is another human—but the best thing for your nervous system is also another human.

In our research, the people who were the best at coping with microstress didn't just find ways to push back, minimize what they caused in others, or rise above. They also made a conscious effort to shape their lives to have more diverse connections with people. They pursued activities, common interests, and group experiences that helped create a rich, multidimensional life to "inoculate" them from microstress's effects. For example, something as simple as meeting friends for a weekly basketball game, or maintaining a group chat to share silly memes that only your closest friends from college will understand, can offer moments of authentic connection that soften the blow of microstresses.

There's a physiological foundation for why. "Engaging with other people . . . trains your brain—like training a coordinated group of muscles—to develop brain circuits for managing your own reactions, responses, and emotions," says neurologist Salinas. There's also a healthy distraction component, because emotional burdens don't weigh on you as much when you're immersed in a multidimensional life. "You tend not to ruminate on your problems when you are around other people who engage your full attention in a positive way," Salinas explains.

Engaging with others also helps you get a better sense of how to frame an issue, especially if you can zoom out to see it in context. You're more likely to be able to say, "I'm not the only person who has had this experience," or, "Other people have it much worse than I do." That kind of perspective can help rightsize microstress.

Additionally, having a multidimensional life means that our identities aren't overly tied to one activity—such as work. Research suggests that high achievers in their twenties and early thirties are often vulnerable to burnout because they haven't developed other dimensions, Salinas says. "Their identities become more and more anchored on their jobs. That means the positive things at work can bring extreme highs, but the negative things can bring extreme lows." The mere act of connecting with others, having informal conversations, sharing mutual interests, or seeing the world from another perspective is a powerful antidote to the daily toll of microstress. But as we go through life, we are pulled in so many directions that we tend to let go of the activities and relationships we once enjoyed.

The percentage of people who say they don't have a single close friend has quadrupled in the past 30 years, according to the Survey Center on American Life. Nearly half of those surveyed said they've lost touch with friends over the past year, while nearly one in 10 report having lost touch with most of their friends. That disconnection matters profoundly. Salinas's research demonstrates that having someone who will listen to you when you need to talk is associated with greater cognitive resilience—meaning your brain can function better than it's expected to, relative to the changes it has undergone from physical aging or disease.

Our research suggests that you need a variety of relationships (not only close friends) to help you get through the reality of living with microstress. The most significant effects come from being connected to people who unite around some interest—poetry, religion, singing, tennis, or activism, for example—but who come from different professional, socioeconomic, educational, or age groups. The shared interests tend to create authentic and trusted interactions, and the diversity of perspectives helps expand the way we see the world and our places in it. We are shaped by the people and experiences, and our lives become multidimensional. And yet in spite of how important relationships are to our happiness, many of us let them slip as the years roll by.

People who told us positive life stories, as we mentioned above when introducing the "Rise above" strategy, invariably described having authentic connections with two, three, or four groups outside of work: athletic activities, volunteer work, civic or religious communities, book or dinner clubs, and so on. Often, one of the groups supported physical health through nutrition, mindfulness, and exercise practices. The relationships formed through these groups tended to be surprising connections that might, on paper, seem a mismatch. But they provided something meaningful.

For example, Rob is an avid cyclist and spends long hours pedaling the countryside with like-minded friends. He benefits from the physical health impacts of the exercise and the meditative nature of rhythmic pedaling. But another huge benefit lies in the friendships he has forged with people who would not normally be in his life: an IT executive, a mail carrier, a cardiologist, and a plumber are now among his closest friends. "I have confided in and felt friendship and laughter from these people in a range of ways that of course reduces the experience of stress," he says. "But the interactions also create perspective, because many of the things I get spun up about seem inconsequential when you look at them through the eyes of a plumber or a cardiologist." Research affirms the experiences Rob has cataloged in his work: The right activities bring a diversity to your social world that not only generates the instrumental benefit of close relationships but also helps you develop the ability to avoid getting caught up in small stresses, and keep them in perspective.

. . .

No one is immune to microstress, and our interviews with high performers make its toll clear. But they also shed light on a better path forward. The insights we gained from hundreds of interviews, as well as from Rob's long-term research on collaboration, show us that it's possible to structure your life in ways that not only reduce microstress but also improve your overall well-being and your relationships with friends, family members, and colleagues. You can foster a diverse set of authentic connections that add dimensionality to your life, which, in turn, helps mitigate the effects of microstress. It's a virtuous cycle.

Originally published in February 2023. Reprint H07GXM

How to Build a Broader Network Within Your Company

by Ko Kuwabara, Jiyin Cao,
Soomin Sophie Cho, and Paul Ingram

When we ask executives if their organizations have become more or less diverse in thought over the past several years, the answer is often unanimous. In one way or another, nearly everyone has witnessed an increase in divergent attitudes, perspectives, and values in the workplace—welcome news given decades of research showing that this type of diversity can foster innovation, creativity, and productivity in organizations.

Yet, when we ask the same people if their own professional networks within their organizations have become more diverse, their responses are less resounding: an uninspired mix of "No" and "I don't know." This is hardly surprising. One of the most pervasive human patterns is homophily, or the idea that birds of a feather flock together. Even as our work environments become increasingly diverse, our tendency is to stick with those who think like us, leaving us ever entrenched in homogenous echo chambers that limit our access and exposure to novel ideas and opportunities.

Still, all of us know people who defy these natural tendencies and build networks that cut across cliques and silos, thriving amid an increasing social and professional complexity. These individuals, sometimes called boundary spanners, break down silos inside organizations by actively exploring outside their comfort zones for new ideas and perspectives different from their own, essentially acting as bridges. They understand that diversity brings a richness that cannot be obtained in isolation.

What can we learn from them about building a diverse network? Our research suggests that what separates these people from the rest is not some inborn trait or ability. Rather, it's a belief that what it takes to build relationships with people who think differently is nothing complicated. In fact, it's a growth mindset for overcoming interpersonal differences in values and opinions.

Beliefs That Can Inhibit Networking

People tend to hold beliefs about whether human traits are innate versus acquired, such as the belief that intelligence is either an inborn quality or developed through hard work. Extensive research has shown that whether one holds a fixed or growth mindset can have pervasive consequences for motivation and performance in a given domain. For instance, decades of research by psychologist Carol Dweck has shown that children with a fixed mindset about intelligence are less motivated to persist at challenging academic tasks because hard work is meaningless if intelligence is believed to be innate. Moreover, these

Idea in Brief

The Challenge

Having a broad network within your company can help you access diverse perspectives, foster collaboration, and open up new opportunities. However, many professionals struggle to expand their connections beyond their immediate team or department.

The Solution

To build a stronger network, identify key individuals to connect with across different departments and levels, then be proactive about reaching out, offering them help, and showing genuine interest in their work. Engaging in cross-functional projects, attending company events, and participating in internal forums or interest groups can also be useful.

The Payoff

A well-developed internal network strengthens your reputation, enhances your ability to influence, and increases your access to information and resources.

children come to value easy wins rather than effortful learning in something new and challenging.

Applying this concept to a workplace context, we hypothesized that people hold either a fixed or growth mindset about building workplace relationships. The intuition is that people with a fixed mindset about these relationships believe in natural compatibility or chemistry; that is, compatible people will just click or get along with one another naturally and effortlessly. Like hopeless singles searching for love at first sight, people with a fixed mindset about personal relationships tend to pursue relationships that come naturally or easily based on immediate rapport and mutual understanding. They don't consider that with work they can develop meaningful and worthwhile relationships when those immediate connections aren't there.

In contrast, for people with a growth mindset, relationships are based first and foremost on effort and commitment—taking the time to get to know one another and learning to overcome differences.

To see how such mindsets affect the diversity of networks people build, we set out to examine relationship formation among 111 working professionals enrolled in an executive MBA program in the United States. We first measured their mindsets using a scale we developed for this project at the beginning of the semester. The scale consisted of five statements, with answers coded from 1 ("strongly disagree") to 6 ("strongly agree"). A higher total score suggested a stronger fixed mindset.

1. Professional relationships are like pieces of a puzzle: People either click or they don't, no matter how little or hard they work at it.

2. The basis of any productive relationship is chemistry, like how naturally and effortlessly you get along with a person.

3. How well you click or get along with a coworker is not something you can control or change easily.

4. A relationship between coworkers without chemistry is likely to not work.

5. A productive relationship is probably not meant to be if it does not develop naturally and effortlessly.

Next, we administered a network survey to see which people each student had developed professional relationships with at the end of the semester. Finally, we measured each person's network diversity by calculating, for each tie formed, how similar or dissimilar the pair is in their personal values (for example, honesty, creativity, risk-taking), as each student reported in a course assignment on self-reflection.

We chose to study networking in a classroom setting because we wanted to understand why some people struggle to build diverse networks in an environment that was designed to be very diverse. Further, it is difficult to study networking in most workplaces, where most people have already built ongoing relationships. Importantly, our subjects were all working managers, not full-time students.

What did we find? As predicted, people with stronger fixed mindsets were less likely to develop ties to others who held dissimilar values. Between the most dissimilar pairs in our sample, people with fixed mindsets were almost 50% less likely than those with growth mindsets to develop ties to people who hold values different from theirs. Conversely, people with fixed mindsets were no more or less likely than their growth-mindset counterparts to develop ties to peers with very similar values. This is a striking demonstration of how personal beliefs and values affect how people network—even when they cannot directly observe one another's values.

Previous research suggests that growth mindsets are particularly important in challenging situations that require effort and perseverance. Among our students, those with a growth mindset who viewed relationships in terms of effort rather than chemistry were more likely to try to bridge interpersonal differences and form diverse networks.

In a follow-up study with 174 MBA students, we set up a classroom experiment to see if different mindsets could be taught and learned on the spot. To this end, students read and reflected on a short article designed to teach either a growth or fixed mindset about relationship building. Next, they were randomly paired to share their personal opinions on workplace politics. After the discussion, students rated how well they worked with each other. The results showed that those induced to have a fixed mindset experienced lower satisfaction when paired with a partner with dissimilar opinions on the case. In contrast, those with an induced growth mindset were equally satisfied regardless of how similar or different they were from their partner.

This study shows that individuals can quickly adopt growth mindsets. While we don't suggest that altering one's mindset alone equates to networking mastery or instant reconciliation with adversaries over political or ideological conflict, examining and adjusting their mindsets could be an accessible yet significant step toward greater inclusion.

Tips for Building Diverse Networks

Based on what we have learned about growth mindsets for relationship building, we offer several recommendations for professionals who want to make their networks stronger, more robust, and more diverse.

Go beyond chemistry

People with a fixed mindset often expect relationships to spring up naturally and spontaneously based on so-called chemistry. Such a viewpoint probably reinforces our natural human tendency—to avoid interpersonal differences—thus exacerbating social isolation and friction in diverse workplaces. The concept of growth mindset suggests a valuable counterpoint. To be boundary spanners and reap the benefits of having a diverse network, first realize it takes deliberate effort and commitment to build relationships. One has to go beyond natural chemistry.

Make it a habit

The idea that it takes deliberate effort over time to build relationships is akin to going to the gym to get fit: No one gets fit by working out only when they feel like it. This means you need to set up a specific time to catch up, seek out opportunities for collaboration, and continually invest effort in understanding and embracing differences. These are valuable strategies for building diverse networks. You'll find that regularly scheduled interactions, not just casual encounters in the canteen or elevator chats, pave the way for deeper rapport and understanding.

Ask questions

The crux of the growth mindset is taking a learning orientation to overcome challenging situations. For instance, instead of perceiving interpersonal differences as obstacles in forming connections, try to see them as opportunities for growth and learning.

Asking questions is one key skill for exercising a growth mindset—not questions to interrogate but to inquire and learn. For instance, in *The Innovator's DNA*, Jeff Dyer, Hal Gregersen, and Clayton Christensen describe one skill that distinguishes truly innovative leaders from ordinary leaders: idea networking, which refers to the intentional practice of engaging with a diverse array of individuals in search of new ideas. By regularly reaching out to people they don't normally interact with and chatting about what they are excited about and what's keeping them up at night, these leaders continue to innovate and inspire. Asking genuine questions about differing viewpoints, values, and experiences plays an important role in nurturing diverse relationships.

. . .

Our research shows that building a diverse network at the workplace starts with changing one's viewpoint about relationship building. We can all adopt a growth mindset, make it a habit to invest effort in embracing differences, and ask genuine questions to better understand one another and nurture relationships.

As workplaces continue to evolve and diversify, the ability to navigate interpersonal differences becomes increasingly crucial. While interpersonal similarity may offer a sense of comfort and familiarity, for individuals, it is imperative to recognize the value of embracing differences and cultivating a growth mindset about professional relationships. For organizations, there's immense value in fostering an environment that encourages individuals to appreciate and respect interpersonal differences, too. Organizations can harness the full potential of diversity, leading to enhanced collaboration, innovation, and overall success.

Adapted from hbr.org, March 6, 2024. Reprint H080J2

8

How to Navigate Conflict with a Coworker

by Amy Gallo

Early in my career I took a job reporting to someone who had a reputation for being difficult. I'll call her Elise. Plenty of people warned me that she would be hard to work with, but I thought I could handle it. I prided myself on being able to get along with anyone. I didn't let people get under my skin. I could see the best in everyone.

Two months later I was ready to quit.

Elise worked long days and on weekends and expected her team to do the same. Her assumptions about what could get done in a day were wildly unreasonable. She often followed up at 8:30 a.m. on a request she'd made at 6:00 the night before. She disparaged my teammates in front of me, questioning their work ethic and commitment to the company. She would scroll through colleagues' calendars and point out how little they'd accomplished despite having a meeting-free day.

I vowed to stop caring so much about how she acted and to treat her with kindness. In a good week I could succeed. But more often than not those lofty intentions flew out the window. The minute she insinuated that I wasn't working hard enough, I would clench my teeth, roll my eyes behind her back, and complain about her to my coworkers.

Interpersonal conflicts like that—with insecure bosses, know-it-all colleagues, passive-aggressive peers—are common at work, and it's easy to get caught up in them. In one study, 94% of respondents said they had worked with a "toxic" person in the previous five years. Another survey—of 2,000 U.S. workers—indicated that their top source of tension on the job was relationships. Trapped in these negative dynamics, we find it hard to be our best selves or to improve the situation. Instead we spend time worrying, react in regrettable ways that violate our values, avoid difficult colleagues, and sometimes even withdraw from work entirely. But those responses can lead to a host of bad outcomes, including reduced creativity, slower and worse decision-making, and even fatal mistakes. For example, as Christine Porath wrote for the *New York Times,* in "a survey of more than 4,500 doctors, nurses and other hospital personnel, 71 percent tied disruptive behavior, such as abusive, condescending or insulting personal conduct, to medical errors, and 27 percent tied such behavior to patient deaths."

None of us is perfect when it comes to navigating the complexity of human relationships. Especially in times of stress, or when we feel threatened, even the most seasoned workplace veterans can find themselves focusing on the short-term goal of ego or reputation protection (*I need to win this argument or to look good in front of my team*) rather than the long-term one of behaving honorably and preserving collegiality.

Idea in Brief

The Problem

Conflict at work is inevitable, but many professionals feel unprepared or uncomfortable handling it—especially when it involves a peer. Misunderstandings, differences in working styles, or misaligned expectations can—when handled badly—damage relationships, reduce collaboration, and hinder performance.

The Solution

Approach conflict with curiosity, empathy, and a problem-solving mindset. Clarify your own goals, listen actively to understand the other person's perspective, be aware of your biases, assume good intent, and work together to find common ground.

The Outcome

With preparation and the right tools, you can transform conflict into an opportunity for stronger collaboration.

So how can we return to our best selves? Having studied conflict management and resolution over the past several years, I've outlined seven strategies that will help you work more effectively with difficult colleagues. These aren't silver bullets that will magically transform your problem coworker into your best friend, but they should make your interactions more tolerable if not more positive. And they'll help you build interpersonal resilience so that you feel less stressed when you're engaged in a conflict and can bounce back from it more quickly.

1. Remember That Your Perspective Is Just One Among Many

We all come to the workplace with different viewpoints and values. We might disagree on everything from whether it's OK to be five minutes late to a meeting to acceptable ways of interrupting a colleague to the appropriate consequences for someone who's made a mistake. It's not realistic to expect your boss, teammates, or reports to see eye to eye with you all the time.

When such differences of opinion arise, however, most of us believe that we're seeing the issue objectively and correctly, and anyone who has another view is uninformed, irrational, or biased. Social psychologists refer to that tendency as *naive realism*. For example, in one study, participants who were asked to tap out the rhythm of a well-known song, such as "Happy Birthday," predicted that listeners would be able to name the tune about 50% of the time. They were sure that it would be clear to others what they were trying to convey. But the guesses were accurate only 2.5% of the time! Once we're confident about something— whether it's our ability to tap out a song or the solution to this quarter's budget shortfall—we find it hard to imagine that others won't see it the same way.

It's important to recognize and resist this gut reaction. Challenge your own perspective by asking questions such as: How do I know that what I believe is true? What if I'm wrong? How would I change my behavior? What assumptions have I made? How would someone with different values and experiences see things? The answers to those questions matter less than the exercise of asking them. They are a good way of reminding yourself that your view is just that: *your view.* Not everyone sees things the same way—and that's OK.

Indeed, you and your colleagues don't need to reach consensus on "the facts" of what's happened or who's to blame for a problem. Instead of spending hours debating whose interpretation is correct, shift your focus to what should happen going forward.

2. Be Aware of Your Biases

Biases creep into all sorts of workplace interactions. One common derailer of colleagues' relationships is *fundamental attribution error*—an inclination to assume that other people's behavior has more to do with their personality than with the situation, while believing the opposite of oneself. For example, you might presume that a teammate who's late to a meeting is disorganized or disrespectful rather than caught in traffic or stuck in another meeting that went long. But when *you're* running behind, you might focus on the circumstances that led to your tardiness.

A related cognitive shortcut that creates problems is *confirmation bias,* or the tendency to interpret events or evidence as proving the truth of existing beliefs. If your view of your colleague Andrew is already negative, you're more likely to interpret his actions as further evidence that he's not up to the task, he's unkind, or he cares only about himself—and it will be increasingly difficult for him to prove you wrong.

Even what we consider difficult behavior can be shaped by the prejudices we carry into the workplace. Earlier in my career I worked with a client—a Black woman—whose ideas I hesitated to challenge, even though that was part of my job as a consultant. I was afraid I'd get a strong reaction, despite the fact that she had never so much as raised her voice in previous encounters. I had fallen into believing the "angry Black woman" stereotype. Now I know to watch out for *affinity bias,* an unconscious tendency to align with people who are similar to us in appearance, beliefs, and background. Research shows that when colleagues aren't like us—in terms of gender, race, ethnicity, education, physical abilities, or position at work—we are less comfortable around them and thus less likely to want to work with them.

How can you interrupt those biases? First, get a better sense of your susceptibility to them by taking an online quiz such as the one from Project Implicit, a nonprofit started by researchers at Harvard, the University of Washington, and the University of Virginia. When you're struggling with a coworker, ask yourself, What role could my biases be playing here? Is it possible I'm not seeing the situation clearly because I'm making assumptions about this person, or unwilling to rethink my initial impression, or unconsciously focusing on our differences?

Play devil's advocate and question your own interpretation of the situation. I learned the "flip it to test it" approach from a TEDx talk by Kristen Pressner, the global head of human resources at a multinational firm: If your colleague was a different gender, race, or sexual orientation or had a different place in the hierarchy, would you make the same assumptions? Would you say the same things or treat that person the same way?

Finally, ask someone you trust—and who will tell you the truth—to help you reflect on the ways in which you might be seeing the situation unfairly.

3. Don't Make It "Me Against Them"

In a disagreement it's easy to think in polarizing ways: "me versus you," enemies at war. One person is being difficult; the other isn't. One person is right; the other is wrong.

To break out of that mental model, instead imagine that there are not two but three entities in the situation: you, your colleague, and the dynamic between you. Maybe that third entity is something specific: a decision you must make together or an assignment you need to complete. Or maybe it's more general: ongoing tension or rivalry between you or bad blood over a project gone wrong. Rather than work to change your colleague, try to make progress on that third thing.

Take Andre, who was struggling with his colleague Emilia. Whenever he proposed a new idea, she produced a list of reasons why it would never work. For a long time Andre saw the two of them as opponents. When I asked how he pictured their dynamic, he told me he saw a dark cloud over her head and a bright sun over his. But that visualization reinforced his view of the situation, prompting him to brace for battle every time he spoke with her. Eventually he decided to shift to less-antagonistic thinking. He started to picture the conflict between them as a seesaw. Though they sat on opposite ends, they could perhaps work together to find balance. That helped him view her as a collaborator rather than an adversary.

No one wants to have a nemesis at work. So think of problematic coworkers as colleagues with whom you share a problem to be solved.

4. Know Your Goal

To avoid drama and stay focused on the work, you need to be clear about your goals. Do you want to get a project over the finish line? Build a healthy working relationship that will last into the future? Feel less angry or frustrated after your interactions?

Make a list of your goals (big and small) and then circle the most important ones. Your intentions will determine—consciously and subconsciously—how you act. For instance, if your goal is to avoid getting stuck in long discussions with a pessimistic colleague, you'll need to take actions different from those you'd take if your goal was to keep the person's nay-saying from bringing down the team.

It's fine to set your sights low. Often it's enough to focus on just having a functional relationship—getting to a point where your skin doesn't crawl when Ethan's name shows up in your inbox or you're not losing sleep at night because Marjorie is making your life miserable. Multiple and more-ambitious goals are OK too. For example, if you're arguing with your insecure boss about which metrics to report to the senior leadership team, your goals might be to: (1) come up with stats that you can both live with, (2) make sure the senior team knows about your expertise, and (3) find a way to avoid heated disagreements before big meetings in the future.

Once you've decided what you want to accomplish, write it down on a piece of paper. Research has shown that people who vividly describe or picture their goals are 1.2 to 1.4 times as likely to achieve them, and that objectives recorded by hand are more likely to be realized. Refer to your goals before interacting with your colleague to keep your eyes on the prize.

5. Avoid Workplace Venting and Gossip—Mostly

It's natural to turn to others when something is off at work. You might want to confirm that you're not misinterpreting a vague email, get advice on advancing a stalled initiative, or simply be reassured that you're a good person. And if your colleague says, "Yes, Greta does seem grumpy. What's up with that?" you get a little jolt of relief: *It's not just me.*

That type of side conversation, whether it happens digitally or in person, can be considered venting. But you might also call it gossip. Despite its bad rap, research shows, gossip can play an important role in bonding with coworkers. When you learn that Marina in marketing also finds Michael in finance difficult and knows of others who feel the same, it fosters a sense of connection. You've essentially formed an in-group that has information that others, especially Michael, don't. And Marina's validation of your perspective gives you a rush of feel-good adrenaline and dopamine.

Studies have also shown that gossip can be beneficial in deterring people from behaving selfishly. If difficult colleagues realize that others are speaking badly of them and warning teammates about working with them, they're more likely to change their ways.

Of course, there are also dangers to venting and gossiping. First, they heighten the risk of confirmation bias. Sure, Michael may be exasperating sometimes, but once you and your work friends start talking about it, you're more likely to interpret his future actions in a negative light. Occasional missteps are painted as an inherent trait, and the "Michael is difficult" storyline becomes entrenched. Second, gossiping often reflects poorly on the gossiper. Although you may get the immediate validation you're seeking, you may also get a reputation for being unprofessional—or end up labeled as the difficult one.

It is perfectly legitimate to seek help with sorting out your feelings or to check with someone else that you're seeing things clearly. But choose whom you talk to (and what you share) carefully. Look for people who are constructive, have your best interests at heart, will challenge your perspective when they disagree, and can be discreet.

6. Experiment to Find What Works

There isn't one right way to get a know-it-all to stop being condescending or your passive-aggressive colleague to deal with you in a more straightforward way. The strategies you choose will depend on the context: who you are, who the other person is, the nature of your relationship, the norms and culture of your workplace, and so on.

Start by coming up with two or three methods you want to test out. Often small actions can have a big impact. Then design an experiment: Determine what you'll do differently, pick a period of time to try it out, and see how it works. For example, if you want to improve communication with a difficult colleague, you might decide that for two weeks you're going to ignore that person's tone and focus on the underlying message. Don't assume the tactic will fix everything wrong between you; view it as an experiment that will teach you something, even if it's only that the approach doesn't work.

Keep trying, tweaking, and refreshing experiments or abandoning ones that don't produce results. For example, if you've tried to handle a colleague's lack of follow-through by sending post-meeting emails that confirm what everyone has agreed to do, but the person still fails to keep promises, then don't keep sending the emails expecting different results. Try something else. As the conflict expert Jennifer Goldman-Wetzler explains, you'll need to find another way to "interrupt the conflict pattern of the past"—often by doing something the other person doesn't expect.

7. Be—and Stay—Curious

Salvador Minuchin, an Argentine therapist, wrote, "Certainty is the enemy of change." When dealing with a negative coworker, it's easy to think, *It's always going to be this way* or *That person will never change*. But resignation and pessimism will get you nowhere. Instead, adopt a curious mindset and maintain hope that your troubled relationship can be improved.

Research shows that curiosity brings a host of benefits: It wards off confirmation bias, prevents stereotyping, and helps us approach tough situations not with aggression (fight) or defensiveness (flight) but with creativity. The key is to shift from drawing often unflattering conclusions to posing genuine questions. When your colleague Jada starts complaining that she's doing more work than anyone else on the team, don't think, *Here we go again with Jada's attitude.* Instead ask yourself, What's going on with her? This feels familiar, but what have I missed in the past? Why is she acting like this?

Try to catch yourself in unproductive thought patterns; then step back and take stock, Who gets along well with Jada, and how do they interact with each other? Have there been times when Jada was more pleasant and cooperative? What was different about those situations?

When you hit a rough patch with someone, think about instances at work or elsewhere when you and another person didn't get along at first but were able to get past it, and reflect on those experiences with curiosity. How were you able to persevere? What helped you achieve resolution? Finally, consider exactly what you stand to gain from meeting the goals you've set out to achieve in a work relationship. Project into the future. If you overcome the conflict, what will be different? How will your work life improve?

You can't be certain of what the future holds for you and your colleague, so be curious instead. It may snap you out of a mindset that's keeping you from discovering an unexpected solution to your problem.

. . .

No matter what type of difficult colleague you're dealing with or what you decide to do next, these seven strategies can improve your odds of responding productively, establishing appropriate boundaries, and building stronger, more fulfilling collaborations at work. Sometimes change isn't possible, in which case you'll eventually need to cut your losses in a relationship and focus on protecting your career and well-being. But I've found that with good-faith efforts and hard work, even some of the trickiest interpersonal conflicts can be resolved.

Originally published in September–October 2022. Reprint R2205L

You're Not Powerless in the Face of Impostor Syndrome

by Keith D. Dorsey

I was intimidated for many years in the early part of my board career because I didn't have a business degree and felt underprepared," a female board director once told me. Another director, explaining that she "grew up in the shadows of a plantation," reflected, "It's still very much a white male show, so the fact that I was the first African American female on the board was astounding to me."

As the U.S. practice leader of CEO and board services at Boyden, an executive search firm, I interact with hundreds of aspiring and existing directors. Questions about their qualifications for board service remain a concern for many of the people I talk to, particularly those from underrepresented backgrounds.

My experience aligns with research that shows that high achievers from underrepresented backgrounds often find themselves confronting impostor syndrome, doubting their skills and achievements, or fearing being exposed as a fraud. Women and people of color may be more likely to feel they don't fit in, they're not welcome, and they don't belong.

Impostor syndrome can be crippling mentally and emotionally, drain your energy and attention, and cause you to fall short of the performance you are capable of, thus feeding the cycle of self-doubt. If you experience impostor syndrome, you may explain away your successes by thinking anyone could have done what you did or you just got lucky, or fear that others are mistaken in believing that you're talented. As if that isn't bad enough, when you stumble or face challenges, your self-perceived incompetence looms larger than life—increasing your chance of failure and perpetuating the syndrome.

While awareness of this cycle is helpful, understanding impostor syndrome does little to end it. Instead, you need action. And to take action, you need moxie.

Moxie: A Working Definition

"Moxie" reflects an intensity of motivation and is related to (but distinct from) traits such as grit, self-control, and the ability to overcome procrastination. The term was popularized by a 1920s soft drink advertised to give people vigor, nerve, and pep. After Boston Red Sox player Ted Williams endorsed the drink, the word "moxie" entered the cultural consciousness as shorthand for strength, aggressiveness, skill, and know-how.

In my own research, I've seen that the attributes of moxie—strength of will, self-discipline, and the ability to persist despite challenges—were vital to the success of underrepresented directors. One Latina executive I spoke with described moxie in this way: "I noticed my Black colleagues overcoming the objections coming at them in their careers. Whenever they set goals, they

Idea in Brief

The Challenge

Impostor syndrome affects many professionals, leading to self-doubt and a persistent fear of being exposed as a fraud. These feelings can hinder their performance, career growth, and overall well-being.

The Solution

By understanding impostor syndrome's roots and implementing strategies to combat them, you can regain your confidence and thrive in your professional life. Start by acknowledging and normalizing your feelings. Seek support from mentors, peers, or professional networks; practice self-compassion; and focus on your achievements and strengths. Reframe negative thoughts and challenge the internal narrative that fuels your self-doubt.

The Payoff

Addressing impostor syndrome can lead to improved self-esteem, increased productivity, and greater career satisfaction.

achieved them. They had a 'refuse to lose' mentality. And once I emulated what I saw in them, I rapidly ascended the corporate ladder myself."

The directors I interviewed explained that they neither internalized the obstacles they encountered as personal failures nor externalized them as irreconcilable systemic barriers. In fact, when I asked them to identify the barriers they faced, it took them a while to recall and identify them because they had transformed their obstacles into sources of motivation. It became apparent that moxie was a response to their childhood experiences of racism, sexism, microaggression, and other difficulties.

If you are a woman or person of color and you want to push forward and advance in your career, you will encounter obstacles and experience failure. At these times, you have a choice to make: Will you allow the obstacles and failures to feed impostor syndrome, or will you pick yourself up and use moxie to persist toward your goal?

If you choose moxie, you may not be disappointed. In a study by psychology professor Jessica Curtis and colleagues, moxie was found to predict intrinsic and extrinsic motivation more than other motivational constructs like grit or self-control. Moxie also predicted goal achievement—largely because people with moxie invest more resources into their aims. For example, one director I interviewed realized that her career choice of spending years as a consultant and then becoming CEO of a small company created substantial obstacles to her landing a corporate board seat. "Boards still tend to recruit against a checklist of wanting a sitting CEO of a multinational corporation," she explained. "So when I'd approach recruiters, they would push back with, 'Ooo . . . ah . . . I'll *really* have to convince the board that it is worth it for them to speak with you.'" At this point, she could have agreed with others' opinions that she wasn't boardroom material. Instead, she recognized the need to translate her experiences and skills into language a board would understand and find attractive. Now, only a few years into board service, she sits on three publicly traded company boards and three nonprofit boards.

Making Moxie Your Superpower

Based on the experiences of the underrepresented directors I interviewed in my study and the aspiring and existing directors I continue to interact with, I suggest four tactics to help you make moxie your very own superpower:

1. Use the strengths you've forged through culture-based hardships

People of color have endured centuries of hardship and oppression, and through these we have forged attitudes and approaches that give us unique advantages, as research regarding racism-related coping and post-traumatic growth following racial trauma has shown. Tabitha Grier-Reed and colleagues at the University of Minnesota have found that deepening your connections with others, harnessing your inner strengths, developing fresh perspectives and appreciation for life, and connecting with your spirituality, in particular, help you grow and flourish in your career and life.

One Black woman board member I interviewed explained that her grandparents had raised her to understand the inequity of opportunities presented to people of color. As a result, she persisted through barriers because, as she put it, "I had no choice. Like other women of my generation, we were told by our parents and grandparents to just get out there and do it. Make it happen. If you're given an opportunity, demonstrate to them that you deserve the opportunity." Similarly, the other directors I interviewed explained that they learned to ignore, go under, go over, go around, or go through any obstacles put in front of them—in other words, they used moxie.

To turn your own hardships into moxie, identify a challenging situation from your past that you ultimately overcame. Reflect on how you got through it and how you resolved the situation. Finally, articulate the principles you learned and the strengths you gained. Together, these are some ingredients of your unique brand of moxie.

For example, women and students of color commonly report facing negative stereotypes when enrolling in STEM courses. One such woman recalled, "I had to take organic chemistry, but without the years of preparatory courses all my classmates had. So I had lots of questions that seemed very elementary to others. As a result, everyone—students, lecturers, and my mentor—thought I didn't belong there and refused to help me." To overcome this formidable challenge, she explained, "I spent many sleepless nights reading extra material, going over class notes and homework multiple times, and slowly caught up. I ultimately graduated from my degree program with one of the highest grades." From this experience, this young woman recognized that she relished challenge and could rely on her strengths of a strong work ethic, self-discipline, focus, and ability to learn unfamiliar, scientific material with limited support. This moxie continued to help her flourish in her career.

2. Give yourself permission to play

Herminia Ibarra, a professor at London Business School, has conducted extensive research on what she calls "identity play," which involves experimenting with new ideas and behaviors as you take on new professional challenges and roles. She uses the term "play" to normalize the idea that you won't perform as well in the new role as you do in more familiar roles.

Importantly, play is not a "fake it till you make it" situation. Instead, it's about authentically growing into new roles by trying new behaviors, gaining confidence, and allowing yourself time and space for development. This was a critical tactic for one director I interviewed, who explained, "Debt financing, bond markets, and the investor base were foreign concepts to me. So when these came up, I reminded myself that I had to have just enough knowledge to stay on the stage, and I kept trying and focused on being a learner."

To foster your own identity play, think of a work situation where you are still on a learning curve. Break the situation or role into a series of small learning experiences where you plan deliberate action, experiment, and gather data on your performance. Then repeat the cycle.

3. Tune out the naysayers

If you are working hard to achieve much in your career and life, you are bound to encounter naysayers who are more than eager to point out the ways you don't measure up. The late Kaleel Jamison, a pioneering career woman in 1970s corporate America, called these messages "nibbles" intended to make you smaller.

When you agree with the nibble (or, worse, initiate the nibble yourself), you feed the impostor syndrome. I recently witnessed this in a young and talented mentee of mine who has been spearheading transformative change in her company despite having taken her role only months ago. While her proposed initiative had been blessed by her boss and her CEO, another leader above her blocked her by saying, "Well, your plan is completely unworkable." She slid into a pit of paralyzing self-doubt. Having seen the plan myself, I knew the criticism was unfounded but suspected there was more to the story. Once we debriefed on the situation, I realized that she had circulated her plan in a way that inadvertently criticized the leader's work, resulting in a predictable backlash. We discussed more-effective ways to solicit support from the various stakeholders involved—including the leader in question. She then created and implemented a more successful approach, in turn, learning from this experience and strengthening her competencies.

When you experience criticism, begin by reframing it as a hypothesis (for example, "The plan will not work"). Next, identify ways to test the hypothesis, such as getting feedback from trusted mentors or conducting a low-risk proof of concept. Third, gather data and test the hypothesis. Regardless of the results, you will gain concrete and actionable feedback that will help you progress.

4. Recognize when to walk away

Impostor syndrome often is used to mask systemic bias and racism in the workplace, as Ruchika Tulshyan and Jodi-Ann Burey aptly noted. This means that moxie won't work in every situation.

One director I interviewed had a long-standing dream to become the CEO at her employer. She came to see, though, that achieving it would take more than her moxie alone: "I eventually realized that even though I was performing well, I couldn't control how the leadership decided who actually got C-suite opportunities and who didn't. So, I made the hard decision that I still wanted to be a CEO, but it didn't have to be there. And I left."

When you encounter an obstacle, take time to assess the competencies, energy, and passion you would need to overcome it and then soberly evaluate whether you want to invest your resources in this way. For example, if you discover that success requires knowledge or skills you don't have and can't realistically develop in the needed time frame, or you can't get the mentoring or advocacy you need to succeed, it may be wiser to walk away. When you deliberately evaluate the obstacles facing you, you will either take on the challenges fully informed or reallocate your abilities in more-suitable environments.

I will be the first to admit that the steps I describe above are not easy. Turning away from impostor syndrome and embracing your moxie requires you to reexamine your assumptions, values, and beliefs; risk new behaviors; and commit more to yourself and your growth than you may ever have before. In other words, embracing moxie sets you on a path of transformative learning, which is rooted in the truism that growth comes from discomfort. As the old man in George Bernard Shaw's *Back to Methuselah* noted, "Life is not meant to be easy, my child, but take courage: it can be delightful."

Adapted from hbr.org, June 2, 2023. Reprint H07N00

9

Feeling Stuck or Stymied?

by Dorie Clark

Time and again, we're reminded that there's no such thing as overnight success. But how long *should* it take us to achieve our career goals? When progress is slower than we'd like, many of us are left wondering: *Is my plan not working—or just not working yet?*

Over the past several years—including during the pandemic's cycles of work frenzy and stagnation—I've researched the question of how we can bring more long-term strategic thinking to our professional lives, despite living in societies that so often glorify high-speed achievement and force us into personal comparisons.

The early-20th-century satirist H. L. Mencken once quipped that success is making at least $100 more a year than your brother-in-law does. But these days, thanks to social media, we're benchmarking ourselves not only against relatives but also against college pals, coworkers, and even celebrity influencers.

When we see some of those people gain recognition early on—by launching unicorn startups, winning coveted prizes and promotions, or making "30 under 30" lists—we forget that they're the exceptions, not the norm.

For many professionals, progress can be frustratingly slow or sputter out unexpectedly. That's common. And yet in these moments a lot of us become dangerously demoralized. Consider Paul Cézanne, whose talents were initially ignored and underappreciated. According to David Galenson, a University of Chicago professor who studies the economics of creativity, Cézanne had "a deep, dark insecurity" as a result. At age 45, a man who would later become an inspiration to young artists—dubbed "the father of us all" by Pablo Picasso—doubted he'd accomplished anything at all.

Businesspeople who hope to build careers in competitive industries, scale up their ventures, or gain recognition in their fields can fall into the same downward spiral. Without a clear understanding of what constitutes a reasonable pace for progress or a way to explain why peers are outachieving them, they may write off promising paths, downsize their plans, or quit altogether. And unlike Cézanne, who slogged on and eventually became a legend, they give up way too soon.

Of course, we shouldn't blindly follow a failing strategy into the grave. But I've found that a lot of professionals make the opposite mistake. They don't allow themselves enough time to succeed. Instead, they need to cultivate "strategic patience." Just as long-term stock investors learn to stand firm on sound ideas during market downturns, people can learn to calmly evaluate the evidence and persevere even when the result isn't guaranteed.

But doing so requires more than following the standard—and passive—advice to just be patient. You need to be both thoughtful

Idea in Brief

The Problem

Career success is often nonlinear. Even ambitious, driven professionals can hit a plateau and be unsure of how to reach the next level, leaving them frustrated and demoralized.

The Solution

Adopt a long-term mindset. Recognize that success often takes longer than expected, and focus on cultivating strategic patience. Invest in your future self by continuing to learn, build relationships, and plant seeds that will bear fruit in time.

The Payoff

Taking small, methodical steps in the direction you want to go—and being willing to wait if you don't get there right away—can help you reach almost any goal.

and proactive. A good way to do that is with a five-step approach involving periodic reassessments and realistic timelines, which helps you lay the groundwork for eventual success.

Research the Target and Terrain

In his 2018 letter to Amazon shareholders, Jeff Bezos told a story about a friend of his who had hired—wait for it—a handstand coach. The coach informed her that most people think they should be able to do a handstand with two weeks' consistent practice. But it actually takes more like *six months'* effort—a stunning 12-fold difference in perception versus reality. If you're under the impression that a target is 12 times easier to achieve than it actually is, it's perfectly rational to give up after a month of trying, thinking you just don't have what it takes. Of course, the problem isn't you or your skills. It's expecting the impossible.

Just like aspiring handstanders, most of us are fairly clueless about what the path to success in our careers actually looks like. Should it take a year? Five years? Fifteen? If you want to become known in your field, do you have to present at 10 conferences, a hundred, or a thousand? If you want to be promoted to team leader, how many stellar performance reviews and project management roles do you need under your belt? If you want the head sales job, which types of clients should you focus on? We often don't know such crucial information and don't realize we're lacking it. So we fixate on unrealistic timelines that can sometimes lead us to despair.

That's why it's important, as you develop and refine your professional objectives, to do research on what has worked for others in the past and make an educated estimate about how long it will reasonably take you to attain your goals. Conditions may vary, but having a rough baseline is helpful.

Reach out to colleagues who have accomplished what you'd like to and push them to identify the markers along their paths. ("How long did it take you to make your first six-figure sale?" you might ask. "How many prospect meetings had you held? How many phone calls did you have to make to land those meetings?") In most cases, unless these people view you as a direct competitor, they won't object to sharing that information. They may be surprised by the level of detail in your questions and have to refresh their memories, but that's typical because no one else asks about these things—which can give you a competitive advantage.

Mapping the terrain enables you to create checkpoints at which you can reflect on your progress or lack thereof. Say you're a startup founder and you know from your research that successful companies in your industry typically hit $2 million in revenue by the end of year two, but you're 18 months in and your projections are barely half that. That's a sign that you need to shift your approach quickly or perhaps get out of the business. After all, the goal isn't to charge forward with all ambitions. Instead, it's to nurture the right ones, jettison the wrong ones, and avoid giving up too soon on viable initiatives that are simply taking a while to gain traction.

Recognize That Progress Can Be Barely Perceptible

There's a long phase in the development of technologies that improve at an exponential rate (like artificial intelligence, 3D printing, and self-driving cars) in which advances are so minimal that even though they're regularly doubling, it seems as if nothing is happening. Authors Peter Diamandis and Steven Kotler call this period the "deception phase," because it prompts many to prematurely dismiss the technology. But once the advances hit a certain threshold, the improvement curve turns sharply up, and success is stunning and swift. (Think of the transition to digital cameras.) The same principle is true in our careers.

As Derek Sivers, the founder of the music distribution company CD Baby, recounted in one interview, his company didn't take off for four years. "Very often I meet people who start their dream idea, and they're a few months into it and they say, 'It's just not going well!' I'm like, 'It's been a few months! Come on!' When I was three years into CD Baby, it was just me and a guy in my house." By year 10 he had sold the company for $22 million.

I've seen something similar happen with the more than 600 participants who have gone through my online Recognized Expert course, which teaches professionals how to build their reputations and brands. On average it takes them about two to three years of effort to show almost any progress in expanding their platforms, and about five years to show meaningful growth.

That said, in the absence of clear movement toward your goal or even the milestones you've set out, you should be able to find small, motivating wins. I call these "raindrops" of progress. They start out intermittent and barely perceptible—praise from a boss or a client, LinkedIn requests from strangers who have started to hear about your work, an invitation to lead a committee, and the like—and on their own, they're not worth popping open the champagne.

But in the aggregate, they're leading indicators of forward momentum, and they can keep you motivated when progress is slow. For example, one talented executive at a consumer packaged goods company I know was overdue for a promotion, but the pipeline was clogged, and she had to wait for a position to open up. It could have been a frustrating interregnum, but she instead focused on noticing raindrops like being asked to present her innovation plans to top customers—a very high-visibility opportunity—and receiving unsolicited praise from the group president. It took longer than she wanted, but thanks to her perseverance, she eventually moved up the ladder.

Leverage Your Relationships in the Right Way

It's human to mark our progress by comparing ourselves with others. But that's often a recipe for feeling terrible. We need to clamp down on that pernicious habit and gain strength from our interpersonal relationships instead.

Rather than looking enviously at more-advanced peers and lamenting your own stagnation, remember to contextualize everyone's success. A good example is the golf handicap, which enables an amateur golfer to enjoy a game against a much better player by using a standardized measure that accounts for that player's advantage. Instead of saying, "Tiger Woods beat me by 45 strokes," which is demoralizing, you could focus on the fact that, taking your handicap into account, you played a better game by your standards than he did by his.

For instance, one friend I know used to measure himself against a particular colleague—until he realized that person had a 17-year head start on him. Now he reminds himself that while he's not as successful as his peer today, he's close to the point where the other man was 17 years ago. Taking age, experience, and other relevant data points into consideration is a far saner and gentler way to approach competition.

Another way you can gain from relationships is to surround yourself with trusted advisers and have them help you evaluate your progress and determine if it's time to pivot. When you're wrapped up in pursuing a certain goal, it's not uncommon to lose perspective and either cling to a failing approach or despair too quickly about a viable one that's percolating slowly. That's why a reality check from a trusted colleague is so necessary.

Elena Akhmetova discovered that several years ago, when she took on a new role within a global tech company. Her mandate was to build an organizational structure from scratch for a critical 250-person department. Three months into the project, after she'd hit repeated roadblocks, her motivation waned: *Was she on the right track? Was she even doing something useful?* She turned to her senior vice president, with whom she had a long-standing relationship. He gave her practical guidance about how to adjust her approach. But even more important, she says, "He told me that this role was so critical now, and there was no other leader who could take it." It was "recognition, respect, and support, all together, and of course, I was able to finish the project."

Stop Moving Your Goalposts

There's a term in environmental science—*shifting baseline syndrome*—that refers to the tendency to change the reference point or norms we measure something against. A scientist, for example, might look at the decline of a species over the length of her career, rather than over the past several hundred years, which would create a distorted perspective.

A similar kind of phenomenon affects the way many professionals evaluate their career trajectories. Over time they get used to their success and begin to take it for granted. One colleague, for instance, says that when she began a collaboration with a major figure in her industry, "the first time I was in the room with him, it felt massive." Nowadays, she says, "it's not exactly humdrum, but it feels normal. I'm a little bit onto the next thing."

She's far from alone. Because we're often so fixated on large-scale goals (the promotion, the invitation to be a keynote speaker, the industry award), we write off some achievements as no big deal, forgetting that five years—maybe even a year—before they would have felt like huge accomplishments. When we keep moving the goalposts, we distort and erase the progress we've already made, which obviously feels discouraging and makes us far more susceptible to quitting. But if we can instead notice and honor where we started and how far we've come, it inspires us to keep moving forward.

Aim for "Directionally Correct"

It's rare that any of us will attain everything in the exact form we predicted. Circumstances change over time (your spouse receives a compelling overseas job offer), and some possibilities are blocked to you through no fault of your own (your company was acquired and your role got eliminated). Instead of dogmatically pursuing one goal, consider striving to make directional progress.

When I was in my early twenties, my goal was to become a university professor. So I dutifully took my GREs and applied to multiple doctoral programs. I was rejected by every single one. It was a devastating setback at the time, but within two years I managed to find a side door. As a fallback I had become a journalist, and with some casual networking through my new job, I managed to land a gig teaching a mass media course at a local university—without the years of study or the expense of a PhD. Nearly 20 years later I still teach, now at several top business schools.

Similarly, Dayna Del Val knew her calling: to become a successful film actress. But faced with an unexpected pregnancy after college, she instead decided to stay near family and raise her son. Her home—near the border of North Dakota and Minnesota—wasn't exactly Hollywood North. But she didn't give up on her ambitions. She tried out for regional acting gigs, eventually landing a signature role as the face of North Dakota in the state's tourism campaign. Del Val's visibility as an actress led to something else unexpected: a position at a local arts nonprofit. For a decade she has served as its CEO, quadrupling its budget and its ability to support the regional arts community.

Del Val didn't become the next Meryl Streep, but she nonetheless carved a meaningful path for herself. "I had a way bigger career than many of my friends who moved to New York or Los Angeles," she says. They often spent years getting rejected at casting calls and never found work they loved, while she thrived in her local creative ecosystem.

None of us can predict every turn our careers or lives will take. We also probably won't land every job we apply for or win every laurel we seek. But that doesn't mean we can't craft a uniquely satisfying, directionally correct form of professional success.

. . .

Let's face it: Patience is annoying. It would be far better if we didn't need it at all and could achieve everything we wanted quickly. But the truth is, in almost all cases, our most meaningful goals require effort and perseverance—and time.

You might need to write a blog few people read as a way to test your ideas and slowly build an audience; take a Toastmasters class when it seems as if no one cares what you have to say, to become a more effective presenter; or spend your lunch hour taking an online course on new developments in your field. You might have to keep making the effort, even when it seems pointless, boring, or hard. There will be dark moments when it's unclear whether you're making any progress at all.

But to achieve the outcomes—and build the career—you want, you have to be willing to work the process. With strategic patience and small, methodical steps—taken today, tomorrow, and the day after—almost any goal is attainable.

Originally published in September–October 2021. Reprint R2105L

10

How Will You Measure Your Life?

by Clayton M. Christensen

B efore I published *The Innovator's Dilemma*, I got a call from Andrew Grove, then the chairman of Intel. He had read one of my early papers about disruptive technology, and he asked if I could talk to his direct reports and explain my research and what it implied for Intel. Excited, I flew to Silicon Valley and showed up at the appointed time, only to have Grove say, "Look, stuff has happened. We have only 10 minutes for you. Tell us what your model of disruption means for Intel." I said that I couldn't—that I needed a full 30 minutes to explain the model, because only with it as context would any comments about Intel make sense. Ten minutes into my explanation, Grove interrupted: "Look, I've got your model. Just tell us what it means for Intel."

I insisted that I needed 10 more minutes to describe how the process of disruption had worked its way through a very different industry, steel, so that he and his team could understand how disruption worked. I told the story of how Nucor and other steel minimills had begun by attacking the lowest end of the market—steel reinforcing bars, or rebar—and later moved up toward the high end, undercutting the traditional steel mills.

When I finished the minimill story, Grove said, "OK, I get it. What it means for Intel is . . . ," and then went on to articulate what would become the company's strategy for going to the bottom of the market to launch the Celeron processor.

I've thought about that a million times since. If I had been suckered into telling Andy Grove what he should think about the microprocessor business, I'd have been killed. But instead of telling him what to think, I taught him how to think—and then he reached what I felt was the correct decision on his own.

That experience had a profound influence on me. When people ask what I think they should do, I rarely answer their question directly. Instead, I run the question aloud through one of my models. I'll describe how the process in the model worked its way through an industry quite different from their own. And then, more often than not, they'll say, "OK, I get it." And they'll answer their own question more insightfully than I could have.

My class at HBS is structured to help my students understand what good management theory is and how it is built. To that backbone I attach different models or theories that help students think about the various dimensions of a general manager's job in stimulating innovation and growth. In each session we look at one company through the lenses of those theories—using them to explain how the company got into its situation and to examine what managerial actions will yield the needed results.

On the last day of class, I ask my students to turn those theoretical lenses on themselves, to find cogent answers to three

Idea in Brief

Harvard Business School's Clayton M. Christensen teaches aspiring MBAs how to apply management and innovation theories to build stronger companies. But he also believes that these models can help people lead better lives. In this chapter, he explains how, exploring questions everyone needs to ask. How can I be happy in my career? How can I be sure that my relationship with my family is an enduring source of happiness? And how can I live my life with integrity? The answer to the first question comes from Frederick Herzberg's assertion that the most powerful motivator isn't money; it's the opportunity to learn, grow in responsibilities, contribute, and be recognized. That's why management, if practiced well, can be the noblest of occupations; no others offer as many ways to help people find those opportunities. It isn't about buying, selling, and investing in companies, as many think. The principles of resource allocation can help people attain happiness at home. If not managed masterfully, what emerges from a firm's resource allocation process can be very different from the strategy management intended to follow. That's true in life too: If you're not guided by a clear sense of purpose, you're likely to fritter away your time and energy on obtaining the most tangible, short-term signs of achievement, not what's really important to you. And just as a focus on marginal costs can cause bad corporate decisions, it can lead people astray. The marginal cost of doing something wrong "just this once" always seems alluringly low. You don't see the end result to which that path leads. The key is to define what you stand for and draw the line in a safe place.

questions: First, how can I be sure that I'll be happy in my career? Second, how can I be sure that my relationships with my spouse and my family become an enduring source of happiness? Third, how can I be sure I'll stay out of jail? Though the last question sounds lighthearted, it's not. Two of the 32 people in my Rhodes scholar class spent time in jail. Jeff Skilling of Enron fame was a classmate of mine at HBS. These were good guys—but something in their lives sent them off in the wrong direction.

As the students discuss the answers to these questions, I open my own life to them as a case study of sorts, to illustrate how they can use the theories from our course to guide their life decisions.

One of the theories that gives great insight on the first question—how to be sure we find happiness in our careers—is from Frederick Herzberg, who asserts that the powerful motivator in our lives isn't money; it's the opportunity to learn, grow in responsibilities, contribute to others, and be recognized for achievements. I tell the students about a vision of sorts I had while I was running the company I founded before becoming an academic. In my mind's eye I saw one of my managers leave for work one morning with a relatively strong level of self-esteem. Then I pictured her driving home to her family 10 hours later, feeling unappreciated, frustrated, underutilized, and demeaned. I imagined how profoundly her lowered self-esteem affected the way she interacted with her children. The vision in my mind then fast-forwarded to another day, when she drove home with greater self-esteem—feeling that she had learned a lot, been recognized for achieving valuable things, and played a significant role in the success of some important initiatives. I then imagined how positively that affected her as a spouse and a parent. My conclusion: Management is the most noble of professions if it's practiced well. No other occupation offers as many ways to help others learn and grow, take responsibility and be recognized for achievement, and contribute to the success of a team. More and more MBA students come to school thinking that a career in business means buying, selling, and investing in companies. That's unfortunate. Doing deals doesn't yield the deep rewards that come from building up people.

I want students to leave my classroom knowing that.

Create a Strategy for Your Life

A theory that is helpful in answering the second question—How can I ensure that my relationship with my family proves to be an enduring source of happiness?—concerns how strategy is defined and implemented. Its primary insight is that a company's strategy is determined by the types of initiatives that management invests in. If a company's resource allocation process is not managed masterfully, what emerges from it can be very different from what management intended. Because companies' decision-making systems are designed to steer investments to initiatives that offer the most tangible and immediate returns, companies shortchange investments in initiatives that are crucial to their long-term strategies.

Over the years I've watched the fates of my HBS classmates from 1979 unfold; I've seen more and more of them come to reunions unhappy, divorced, and alienated from their children. I can guarantee you that not a single one of them graduated with the deliberate strategy of getting divorced and raising children who would become estranged from them. And yet a shocking number of them implemented that strategy. The reason? They didn't keep the purpose of their lives front and center as they decided how to spend their time, talents, and energy.

It's quite startling that a significant fraction of the 900 students that HBS draws each year from the world's best have given little thought to the purpose of their lives. I tell the students that HBS might be one of their last chances to reflect deeply on that question. If they think that they'll have more time and energy to reflect later, they're nuts, because life only gets more demanding: You take on a mortgage; you're working 70 hours a week; you have a spouse and children.

For me, having a clear purpose in my life has been essential. But it was something I had to think long and hard about before I understood it. When I was a Rhodes scholar, I was in a very demanding academic program, trying to cram an extra year's worth of work into my time at Oxford. I decided to spend an hour every night reading, thinking, and praying about why God put me on this earth. That was a very challenging commitment to keep, because every hour I spent doing that, I wasn't studying applied econometrics. I was conflicted about whether I could really afford to take that time away from my studies, but I stuck with it—and ultimately figured out the purpose of my life.

Had I instead spent that hour each day learning the latest techniques for mastering the problems of autocorrelation in regression analysis, I would have badly misspent my life. I apply the tools of econometrics a few times a year, but I apply my knowledge of the purpose of my life every day. It's the single most useful thing I've ever learned. I promise my students that if they take the time to figure out their life purpose, they'll look back on it as the most important thing they discovered at HBS. If they don't figure it out, they will just sail off without a rudder and get buffeted in the very rough seas of life. Clarity about their purpose will trump knowledge of activity-based costing, balanced scorecards, core competence, disruptive innovation, the four Ps, and the five forces.

My purpose grew out of my religious faith, but faith isn't the only thing that gives people direction. For example, one of my former students decided that his purpose was to bring honesty and economic prosperity to his country and to raise children who were as capably committed to this cause, and to each other, as he was. His purpose is focused on family and others—as mine is.

The choice and successful pursuit of a profession is but one tool for achieving your purpose. But without a purpose, life can become hollow.

Allocate Your Resources

Your decisions about allocating your personal time, energy, and talent ultimately shape your life's strategy.

I have a bunch of "businesses" that compete for these resources: I'm trying to have a rewarding relationship with my wife, raise great kids, contribute to my community, succeed in my career, contribute to my church, and so on. And I have exactly the same problem that a corporation does. I have a limited amount of time and energy and talent. How much do I devote to each of these pursuits?

Allocation choices can make your life turn out to be very different from what you intended. Sometimes that's good: Opportunities that you never planned for emerge. But if you misinvest your resources, the outcome can be bad. As I think about my former classmates who inadvertently invested for lives of hollow unhappiness, I can't help believing that their troubles relate right back to a short-term perspective.

When people who have a high need for achievement—and that includes all Harvard Business School graduates—have an extra half hour of time or an extra ounce of energy, they'll unconsciously allocate it to activities that yield the most tangible accomplishments. And our careers provide the most concrete evidence that we're moving forward. You ship a product, finish a design, complete a presentation, close a sale, teach a class, publish a paper, get paid, get promoted. In contrast, investing time and energy in your relationship with your spouse and children typically doesn't offer that same immediate sense of achievement. Kids misbehave every day. It's really not until 20 years down the road that you can put your hands on your hips and say, "I raised a good son or a good daughter." You can neglect your relationship with your spouse, and on a day-to-day basis, it doesn't seem as if things are deteriorating. People who are driven to excel have this unconscious propensity to underinvest in their families and overinvest in their careers—even though intimate and loving relationships with their families are the most powerful and enduring source of happiness.

If you study the root causes of business disasters, over and over you'll find this predisposition toward endeavors that offer immediate gratification. If you look at personal lives through that lens, you'll see the same stunning and sobering pattern: people allocating fewer and fewer resources to the things they would have once said mattered most.

Create a Culture

There's an important model in our class called the Tools of Cooperation, which basically says that being a visionary manager isn't all it's cracked up to be. It's one thing to see into the foggy future with acuity and chart the course corrections that the company must make. But it's quite another to persuade employees who might not see the changes ahead to line up and work cooperatively to take the company in that new direction. Knowing what tools to wield to elicit the needed cooperation is a critical managerial skill.

The theory arrays these tools along two dimensions—the extent to which members of the organization agree on what they want from their participation in the enterprise, and the extent to which they agree on what actions will produce the desired results. When there is little agreement on both axes, you have to use "power tools"—coercion, threats, punishment, and so on—to secure cooperation. Many companies start in this quadrant, which is why the founding executive team must play such an assertive role in defining what must be done and how. If employees' ways of working together to address those tasks succeed over and over, consensus begins to form. MIT's Edgar Schein has described this process as the mechanism by which a culture is built. Ultimately, people don't even think about whether their way of doing things yields success. They embrace priorities and follow procedures by instinct and assumption rather than by explicit decision—which means that they've created a culture. Culture, in compelling but unspoken ways, dictates the proven, acceptable methods by which members of the group address recurrent problems. And culture defines the priority given to different types of problems. It can be a powerful management tool.

In using this model to address the question, How can I be sure that my family becomes an enduring source of happiness?, my students quickly see that the simplest tools that parents can wield to elicit cooperation from children are power tools. But there comes a point during the teen years when power tools no longer work. At that point parents start wishing that they had begun working with their children at a very young age to build a culture at home in which children instinctively behave respectfully toward one another, obey their parents, and choose the right thing to do. Families have cultures, just as companies do. Those cultures can be built consciously or evolve inadvertently.

If you want your kids to have strong self-esteem and confidence that they can solve hard problems, those qualities won't magically materialize in high school. You have to design them into your family's culture—and you have to think about this very early on. Like employees, children build self-esteem by doing things that are hard and learning what works.

Avoid the "Marginal Costs" Mistake

We're taught in finance and economics that in evaluating alternative investments, we should ignore sunk and fixed costs, and instead base decisions on the marginal costs and marginal revenues that each alternative entails. We learn in our course that this doctrine biases companies to leverage what they have put in place to succeed in the past, instead of guiding them to create the capabilities they'll need in the future. If we knew the future would be exactly the same as the past, that approach would be fine. But if the future's different—and it almost always is—then it's the wrong thing to do.

This theory addresses the third question I discuss with my students—how to live a life of integrity (stay out of jail). Unconsciously, we often employ the marginal cost doctrine in our personal lives when we choose between right and wrong. A voice in our head says, "Look, I know that as a general rule, most people shouldn't do this. But in this particular extenuating circumstance, just this once, it's OK." The marginal cost of doing something wrong "just this once" always seems alluringly low. It suckers you in, and you don't ever look at where that path ultimately is headed and at the full costs that the choice entails. Justification for infidelity and dishonesty in all their manifestations lies in the marginal cost economics of "just this once."

I'd like to share a story about how I came to understand the potential damage of "just this once" in my own life. I played on the Oxford University varsity basketball team. We worked our tails off and finished the season undefeated. The guys on the team were the best friends I've ever had in my life. We got to the British equivalent of the NCAA tournament—and made it to the final four. It turned out the championship game was scheduled to be played on a Sunday. I had made a personal commitment to God at age 16 that I would never play ball on Sunday. So I went to the coach and explained my problem. He was incredulous. My teammates were, too, because I was the starting center. Every one of the guys on the team came to me and said, "You've got to play. Can't you break the rule just this one time?"

I'm a deeply religious man, so I went away and prayed about what I should do. I got a very clear feeling that I shouldn't break my commitment—so I didn't play in the championship game.

In many ways that was a small decision—involving one of several thousand Sundays in my life. In theory, surely I could have crossed over the line just that one time and then not done it again. But looking back on it, resisting the temptation whose logic was "In this extenuating circumstance, just this once, it's OK" has proven to be one of the most important decisions of my life. Why? My life has been one unending stream of extenuating circumstances. Had I crossed the line that one time, I would have done it over and over in the years that followed.

The lesson I learned from this is that it's easier to hold to your principles 100% of the time than it is to hold to them 98% of the time. If you give in to "just this once," based on a marginal cost analysis, as some of my former classmates have done, you'll regret where you end up. You've got to define for yourself what you stand for and draw the line in a safe place.

Remember the Importance of Humility

I got this insight when I was asked to teach a class on humility at Harvard College. I asked all the students to describe the most humble person they knew. One characteristic of these humble people stood out: They had a high level of self-esteem. They knew who they were, and they felt good about who they were. We also decided that humility was defined not by self-deprecating behavior or attitudes but by the esteem with which you regard others. Good behavior flows naturally from that kind of humility. For example, you would never steal from someone, because you respect that person too much. You'd never lie to someone, either.

It's crucial to take a sense of humility into the world. By the time you make it to a top graduate school, almost all your learning has come from people who are smarter and more experienced than you: parents, teachers, bosses. But once you've finished at Harvard Business School or any other top academic institution, the vast majority of people you'll interact with on a day-to-day basis may not be smarter than you. And if your attitude is that only smarter people have something to teach you, your learning opportunities will be very limited. But if you have a humble eagerness to learn something from everybody, your learning opportunities will be unlimited. Generally, you can be humble only if you feel really good about yourself—and you want to help those around you feel really good about themselves, too. When we see people acting in an abusive, arrogant, or demeaning manner toward others, their behavior almost always is a symptom of their lack of self-esteem. They need to put someone else down to feel good about themselves.

Choose the Right Yardstick

This past year I was diagnosed with cancer and faced the possibility that my life would end sooner than I'd planned. Thankfully, it now looks as if I'll be spared. But the experience has given me important insight into my life.

I have a pretty clear idea of how my ideas have generated enormous revenue for companies that have used my research; I know I've had a substantial impact. But as I've confronted this disease, it's been interesting to see how unimportant that impact is to me now. I've concluded that the metric by which God will assess my life isn't dollars but the individual people whose lives I've touched.

I think that's the way it will work for us all. Don't worry about the level of individual prominence you have achieved; worry about the individuals you have helped become better people. This is my final recommendation: Think about the metric by which your life will be judged, and make a resolution to live every day so that in the end, your life will be judged a success.

Originally published in July–August 2010. Reprint R1007B

Discussion Guide

Are you feeling inspired by what you've read in this collection? Do you want to share the ideas in the articles or explore the insights you've gleaned with others? This discussion guide offers an opportunity to dig a little deeper, with questions to prompt personal reflection and to start conversations with your team.

You don't need to have read the book from beginning to end to use this guide. Choose the questions that apply to the articles you have read or that you feel might spark the liveliest discussion.

Reflect on key takeaways from your reading to help you adopt the ideas and techniques you want to integrate into your work as a leader. What tools can you share with your team to help everyone be their best? Becoming the leader you want to be starts with a detailed plan—and a commitment to carrying it out.

1. Name some examples of your professional strengths, preferred ways of working, and values. How did you uncover and identify them? How do you use your understanding of them to make the greatest impact? Do you have any strengths that you don't really enjoy using but have helped you succeed?

2. In "You Don't Find Your Purpose—You Build It," John Coleman talks about building your purpose as opposed to finding it. How would you articulate your personal purpose? How has it evolved over time? What sources of meaning (such as family, work, or community) have helped you build it?

3. Define your personal brand in 30 seconds or less. How have you refined or developed your brand during your career? What jobs, experiences, or expertise has been most important for that?

4. Recall a time when you faced a significant ethical challenge at work. How did you navigate that situation—and were you pleased with your response? As you plan your career going forward, what "eulogy virtues" (things people praise you for after you've died) do you want to be remembered for?

5. How do you cultivate a learning mindset in your daily work? When has that mindset helped you overcome a challenge? What learning goals can you set to ensure you continue growing in your current role?

6. Amy Jen Su writes that you don't need just one leadership voice in your career—you need many voices to use in various situations. What does "leadership voice" mean to you, and what aspects of your character, experience, or expertise influence it? How have you adapted your leadership voice to different contexts?

7. What methods do you use to manage your four kinds of energy (physical, mental, emotional, and spiritual) throughout the workday? How has doing so improved your productivity and well-being? Which of the four kinds of energy could you better manage—and what's getting in the way of that?

8. Which cognitive biases tend to affect you the most often? Describe an example of when cognitive bias influenced

you and what the result was. What tools or approaches could you use to minimize the effects of cognitive bias in the future?

9. How have the three happiness traps (being ambitious, doing what's expected, and overworking) affected how you've navigated your career? What strategies do you use to find meaning and purpose in what you do?

10. What are some examples of microstressors (small sources of stress that accumulate and compound over time) you encounter in your day-to-day life? What effects do they have on your productivity, health, or mood? Which of the practices that Rob Cross and Karen Dillon recommend could you try to reduce their impact?

11. How would you characterize your network within your organization: broad, narrow, diverse, homogenous? When have you successfully dealt with a challenge—or struggled to—because of your network's composition? What could you do to strengthen your network and connect with more colleagues who have different perspectives or backgrounds?

12. Describe a time when you had a conflict with a coworker. What steps did you take to understand your colleague's point of view, identify any biases affecting your perspective, recognize how your behavior was influencing the situation, and approach the conflict as a problem to be solved jointly? How could you do any—or all—of these better in the future?

13. Have you ever experienced impostor syndrome—the feeling that you're a fraud, even when your skills and experience say

otherwise? What happened, and how did it affect your confidence and performance? What methods have you used, or could you use, to combat impostor syndrome?

14. In chapter 9 Dorie Clark writes about the need for "strategic patience" in our careers, because achieving our goals often takes much longer than we expect. Think about the first time you felt like a success—however you defined it. What were the circumstances? How far into your career was it? What can you do to maintain a long-term perspective about meeting your future goals?

15. What do fulfillment and success mean to you, and how do they factor into how you balance your career and personal life? How do you make sure you're putting your time and energy toward what matters most to you?

16. What other sources on managing yourself have had a significant impact on your work? Were there voices or subtopics you missed in this collection? Were there voices or subtopics included that surprised you?

17. After reading and reflecting on this book and discussing it with people on your team, write down the ideas and techniques you want to try. Think of how you might experiment and implement them in both the short term and long term. Draft a plan to move forward.

About the Contributors

Erika Andersen is the founding partner of Proteus International, a coaching, consulting, and training firm that focuses on leader readiness. In addition to her latest book, *Change from the Inside Out*, she is the host of the podcast *The Proteus Leader Show* and the author of four previous books: *Growing Great Employees, Being Strategic, Leading So People Will Follow*, and *Be Bad First*.

Jiyin Cao is an associate professor at the School of Management and Economics and the Shenzhen Finance Institute, the Chinese University of Hong Kong, Shenzhen. She received her PhD from the Kellogg School of Management. Her research focuses on trust, culture, and the psychological processes underlying social network formation and decay.

Soomin Sophie Cho is an assistant professor in the Organisations and Innovation Group at the University College London School of Management. She received her PhD in management from Columbia Business School. Her research interests lie in the areas of culture, entrepreneurship, and diversity.

Clayton M. Christensen was the Kim B. Clark Professor of Business Administration at Harvard Business School and a frequent contributor to *Harvard Business Review*.

Dorie Clark is a marketing strategist and professional speaker who teaches at Columbia Business School. She is the author of

Entrepreneurial You, Stand Out, Reinventing You, and *The Long Game.*

John Coleman is the author of the *HBR Guide to Crafting Your Purpose* (Harvard Business Review Press, 2022).

Rob Cross is the Edward A. Madden Professor of Global Leadership at Babson College in Wellesley, Massachusetts, and a senior vice president of research at the Institute for Corporate Productivity. He is a coauthor of *The Microstress Effect* (Harvard Business Review Press, 2023) and the author of *Beyond Collaboration Overload* (Harvard Business Review Press, 2021).

Karen Dillon is a former editor of *Harvard Business Review* and a coauthor of *The Microstress Effect* (Harvard Business Review Press, 2023). She is also a coauthor of three books with Clayton Christensen, including the *New York Times* bestseller *How Will You Measure Your Life?*

Keith D. Dorsey is a managing partner and the U.S. practice leader of CEO and board services at Boyden, a global executive search firm with 75 offices in 45 countries. He is a researcher, author, adviser, and active board member at Vimly Benefit Solutions, Pepperdine University's Graziadio Business School, and the City of La Quinta's Financial Advisory Commission.

Peter F. Drucker was an Austrian-born American management consultant, educator, and author whose writings contributed to the philosophical and practical foundations of the modern business corporation. He was also a leader in the development of management education, invented the concept known as management by objectives, and has been described as "the founder of modern management."

Amy Gallo is a contributing editor at *Harvard Business Review*, a cohost of the *Women at Work* podcast, and the author of *Getting Along* (Harvard Business Review Press, 2022) and the *HBR Guide to Dealing with Conflict* (Harvard Business Review Press, 2017). She writes and speaks about workplace dynamics.

Paul Ingram is the Kravis Professor of Business at Columbia Business School. He consults on leadership, organizational design, and strategy to companies around the world.

Maryam Kouchaki is a professor of management and organizations at the Kellogg School of Management. Her research explores ethics, morality, and the complexity and challenges of managing ethnic and gender diversity for organizations.

Ko Kuwabara is an associate professor of organizational behavior at INSEAD Asia in Singapore. His current research focuses on social exchange in the context of networking, including beliefs and misperceptions that derail productive relations and interactions in the workplace. He received his PhD in sociology from Cornell University.

Catherine McCarthy is a senior vice president at the Energy Project.

Annie McKee is a senior fellow at the University of Pennsylvania Graduate School of Education and the director of the PennCLO Executive Doctoral Program. She is the author of *How to Be Happy* *at Work* (Harvard Business Review Press, 2017) and a coauthor of several books, including *Becoming a Resonant Leader* (Harvard Business Review Press, 2008) with Richard Boyatzis and Fran Johnston.

Katherine L. Milkman is the James G. Campbell Jr. Assistant Professor of Operations and Information Management at the University of Pennsylvania's Wharton School. She is a coauthor of "A User's Guide to Debiasing," a chapter in the *Wiley Blackwell Handbook of Judgment and Decision Making*.

Rachel Montañez is a keynote speaker on burnout and self-advocacy in the workplace. Her clients include a range of *Fortune* companies including Google, General Mills, L'Oréal, and Under Armour. She's lived and worked in the United Kingdom, South Korea, Japan, and her home base, the United States.

John W. Payne is the Joseph J. Ruvane Jr. Professor of Business Administration at Duke University's Fuqua School of Business. He is a coauthor of "A User's Guide to Debiasing," a chapter in the *Wiley Blackwell Handbook of Judgment and Decision Making*.

Tony Schwartz is the CEO of the Energy Project and author of *The Way We're Working Isn't Working*.

Isaac H. Smith is an associate professor of organizational behavior and human resources at the BYU Marriott School of Business. His research explores the morality and ethics of organizations and the people in them.

Jack B. Soll is an associate professor of management at Duke University's Fuqua School of Business. He is a coauthor of "A User's Guide to Debiasing," a chapter in *The Wiley Blackwell Handbook of Judgment and Decision Making.*

Amy Jen Su is a cofounder and managing partner of the Mariswood Group, a boutique executive coaching and leadership development firm. For the past two decades, she has coached CEOs, executives, and rising stars in organizations. She is the author of *The Leader You Want to Be* (Harvard Business Review Press, 2019) and a coauthor of *Own the Room* (Harvard Business Review Press, 2013).

Index